Introduction

Images touch our feelings, and making things helps us to express our inner experiences

'The image educates emotion where reason never reaches. The significant image held, recalled has the power to transform.'

Dorothea Blum (1963), Quaker

Many people of faith regard human beings as both created and creative. Humankind's capacity for appreciating beauty, shape, colour and form leads many to wonder about the nature of the creative power behind the universe and also to want to create things. This link to transcendent experience, and to the transforming power of creativity, makes art and RE true partners in the human search for meaning and understanding.

This *Spirited Arts* pack draws on artwork created by pupils of a variety of ages and backgrounds, and also on more widely known works of art by professional artists. The online gallery at www.pcfre.org.uk/spiritedarts displays more inspirational work by pupils across the UK. Many of the activities suggested in the following pages will enable pupils in primary schools to explore their own creative and artistic talents as they express their learning in RE in new and challenging ways.

Using art-based activities in RE and using art as a resource will appeal to pupils with a variety of preferred learning styles – visual, spatial, kinaesthetic, intrapersonal and logical-mathematical. Teachers and pupils alike are sure to enjoy the visual delights that *Spirited Arts* offers. The chance to get creative is fun and may well reveal the next Michelangelo to be in your classroom!

Rachel Barker

Editor

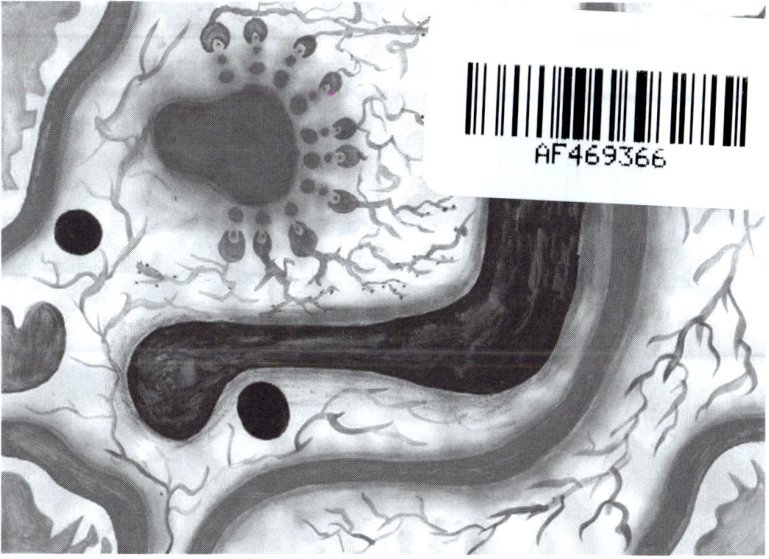

'Art is the desire of a man (sic) to express himself, to record the reactions of his personality to the world he (sic) lives in'

Amy Lowell, poet, 1874–1925

Contents

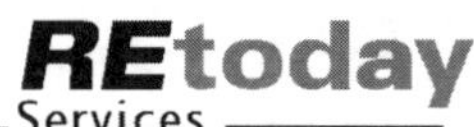

RE and art – art and RE: pedagogy and links

Human beings have responded artistically to their experiences (corporate and individual) throughout time and in all cultures. They have addressed key questions of meaning and purpose, identity and morality by, for example, painting on cave walls, decorating tombs, and creating canvases and sculptures to adorn both private homes and public space. Artists use colour, shape, texture, pattern, size and different materials to communicate what they see, hear, feel, touch, understand, believe and wonder about. People experiencing the artist's work respond to it on different levels– for example, critically, aesthetically and spiritually.

RE and Art

Humankind's spiritual and religious quest is reflected in and through artistic expression of various types. 'Religious' art exists in abundance and in RE can be seen as 'windows' through which religious beliefs and the responses of adherents are seen. As such, to focus on a piece of art which tells a religious story (like the Parable of the Prodigal Son, pages 10-11), or a key experience of a spiritual leader (like the Four Sights of the Buddha, pages 16-17) provides a legitimate 'way into' understanding religious concepts, beliefs and practices and responding to them.

Art and RE

Developing personal responses to the teachings and practices of the religious traditions is an essential element of RE ('learning from religion'). Pupils should be given a variety of creative opportunities to express their personal thoughts, responses and beliefs – orally, in writing and artistically – all based on RE learning outcomes. The art and design curriculum promotes creativity and imagination, helping pupils to process their ideas and make aesthetic judgements. Such skills can be drawn on to provide opportunities for pupils to draw, paint, do collage or sculpt their response to issues raised in RE.

Creative work in RE and in Art

RE and Art are potentially transformational and in them pupils need to be enabled to *engage with experience* (both their own and others') – seeing the relevance of what they are doing, asking questions and seeking answers; to *commit themselves to their work* and 'make it their own', within a safe learning environment in which personal issues can be shared and ideas and responses 'tested'; to *achieve* and be able to *demonstrate success* in a variety of ways.

Promoting creativity in RE and Art

Creativity always involves *thinking or behaving imaginatively and purposefully*; it generates something *original* (either literally or 'new to the person' – facts, understanding, insights) and it is *of value* in relation to its purpose – if it achieves what the teacher/pupil set out to achieve.

Some key questions to ask with regard to promoting creativity

- Has the work a clear purpose? Have I provided a framework but allowed for flexibility in personal ways of working and response?
- How interesting is the material to fire the imagination? Is it 'grounded' in pupils' experience?
- Do I provide them with different ways of working and allow them to work in different groupings? Is the timing (pace) of the task appropriate for them to achieve? What variety do I provide?
- Do I ask, and do I encourage my pupils to ask, open-ended questions and engage in critical reflection? 'What if...?', 'Why is...?' and 'How might...?'

See: 'Excellence and enjoyment':
www.standards.dfes.gov.uk

On the National Curriculum Action website you will find a number of relevant sources e.g. 'Creativity: find it, promote it':
www.ncaction.org.uk/creativity

and in the subjects section examples for RE and Art:
www.ncaction.org.uk/subjects

Spirited Arts: Art in heaven and in the classroom

There have been three competitions for pupils' 'art-in-RE' under the title 'Art in Heaven', run by The Professional Council for Religious Education. Pages 3 to 5 share some of the excellent ideas that teachers have given for the competition in primary RE, and encourages you to try these approaches with your pupils, whether they are 6 or 11. The Art in Heaven web gallery is available at www.pcfre.org.uk/spiritedarts

The eight picture cards included with this booklet are all examples of 'Art in Heaven' work. It's important when using them to get pupils to look carefully. There are three suggestions on this page as to how you might do this.

RE too often models 'respond by regurgitating': 'here is a story from a religion, now feed it back to me'. We can do better! In using art activities, especially for narrative purposes, the task the teacher sets is everything, so let's do away with 'draw a picture' as the framework to the task. This article goes on to suggest four straightforward alternatives which involve 'reflect and respond' rather than 'regurgitate' as their way of working.

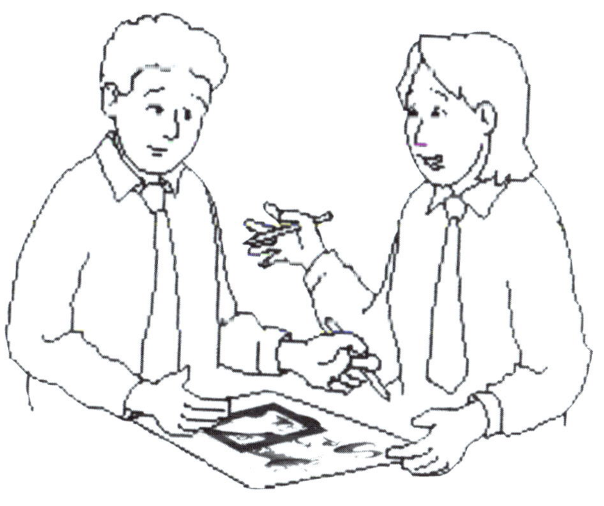

Three observation strategies

- that help learners to view with care.

Use the pictures in this resource or select a range around a particular theme.

1. Gallery

Frame the pictures with large sheets of backing paper and blu-tac them up around the classroom. *For younger pupils*: give out a set of sticky spots numbered 1 to 8 to each pair. Ask them to judge the pictures for a competition. They might begin by guessing the age of the artist in each case. Which do they think is the winner? Put spot 1 next to it. Which deserves a silver medal? Have a class vote to put the pictures in order of merit, and encourage discussion about what is good about each one. *Older pupils* can do the same activity, but work individually. Give them four post-it notes each, and ask them to choose their 'top four' and write a comment on why each is a winner.

2. Image and words

Put pupils in small groups to look at these eight pictures. Ask them to attend to the pupils' comments and the judges' comments on the back – get one person (an able reader) to read these out. Ask the group to write a 50-word explanation of their picture, saying what it shows and why it is good. They can pass on their picture and explanation to another group for discussion.

3. Observation frames

Use a rectangle of card (A5 size is just right) with about one-third cut out of the centre – like a picture frame. Ask pupils in pairs to move the rectangle around on the surface of one of the pictures, looking at what appears in the frame. Ask them some questions about what they see – the colours, the style of the art, the images presented, and other details.

 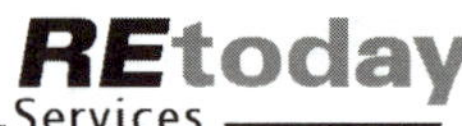

Exciting story - art for RE

Here are four ways of working with stories and pictures in your RE classroom. All these connect effectively with the art curriculum – for example designing and making images and artefacts.

1. Feel safe, feel in danger

This strategy works well with 5–7s, enabling their 'learning from religion' and personal search. Show children the picture card of Emily's 'Parable of the Lost Sheep' as an example.

Take any story from faith – Rama and Sita, the Prodigal Son, Noah's Flood – and ask pupils: Who are the leading characters? When did the leading characters feel in danger? When did they feel safe? Pupils draw two pictures to show a moment of danger and a moment of safety. Then ask them to draw a picture of when they felt in danger, and when they felt safe. This links faith stories to the feelings of the learners in a simple way, and can be adapted to help pupils to develop key skills e.g. 'talking about' (level 1), 'responding sensitively and suggesting meanings' (level 2), 'making links' (level 3) and 'applying ideas' (level 4). It seems to work for most faith stories – is there any story not about faith and danger? There are many examples for pupils to see on the 'Art in Heaven' web gallery: www.pcfre.org.uk/spiritedarts

Safety and danger at the Last Supper

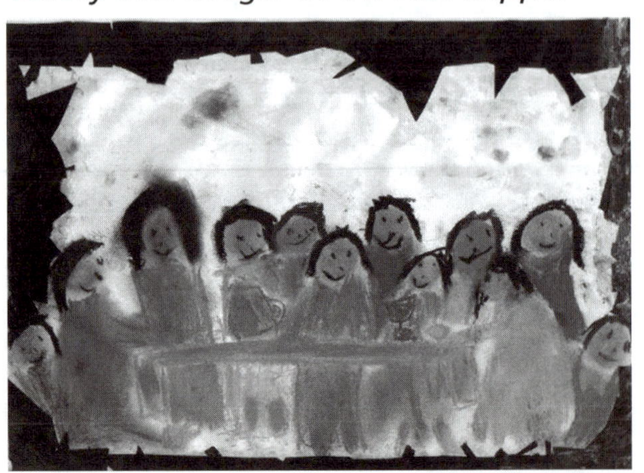

How would your pupils animate the Exodus?

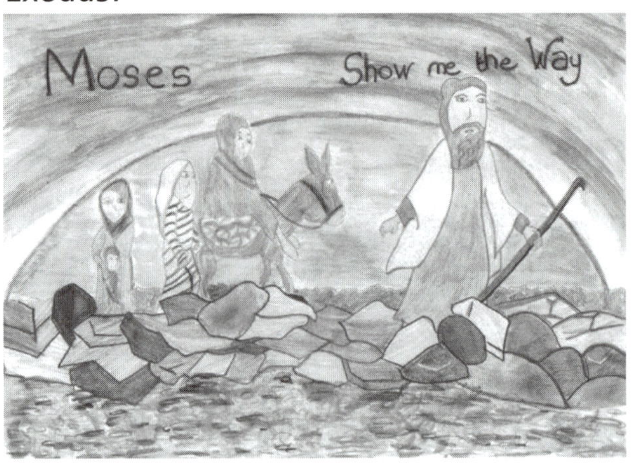

2. Fast storyboards and DVD covers

Take almost any religious story (it is best to avoid Islamic stories of the Prophets, who should not be drawn, and pictures of Sikh gurus should be 2D although some Sikhs prefer their gurus not to be drawn at all), and ask your pupils to be the 'urgent' team at a movie making agency. They have 20 minutes, in 3s, to prepare a presentation for a client, who wants to know 'How would you make a movie out of this story?' They'll need to develop a style and a storyboard (with, say, 12 sketches of the story's key moments in it) that show the unfolding action. Ask 9-year-olds to make a version of the story for 5-year-olds. This forces pupils to think: what are the key moments in the story? Pupils working at level 2 will be able to retell the story, while pupils working at level 4 will be able to show understanding of the story's messages. The follow-up activity is to design the video/DVD cover for the film they've planned. Urge pupils to pick out what makes the story significant, exciting or worth watching. These activities are about the beginnings of interpretation.

3. Islamic Rules

There is great discipline in Islamic art. Allah must not be pictured, and often no human faces are pictured, so artists must think of subtle ways to make art that communicates. This can be a good learning discipline for pupils. Picture card 4 shows Craig and Derya's wonderful images of the revelation of the Holy Qur'an to the Prophet. Pupils from this Special School apply the Islamic rules in their own creative work with real insight.

Take a story or saying of the Prophet. Ask pupils to think in 3 steps: What is the meaning or mood of this story or saying? What images, colours, materials or ideas show this meaning or mood? How can this meaning or mood be shown in a picture that has no image of God or humanity in it? Then they make the art. Ask them to explain about their work using level appropriate prompts e.g:

- Making this picture made me think about… ('Respond sensitively' – level 2)
- Islamic rules for art are… ('Describe' – level 3)
- My picture uses Islamic art rules because… ('Apply ideas' – level 4)

Revelation placed into the Prophet's hand – an example of 'Islamic rules' artwork

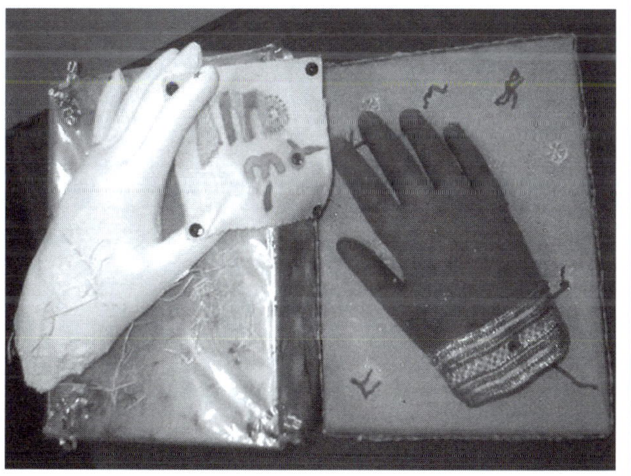

This image of Pentecost shows much more than the biblical story

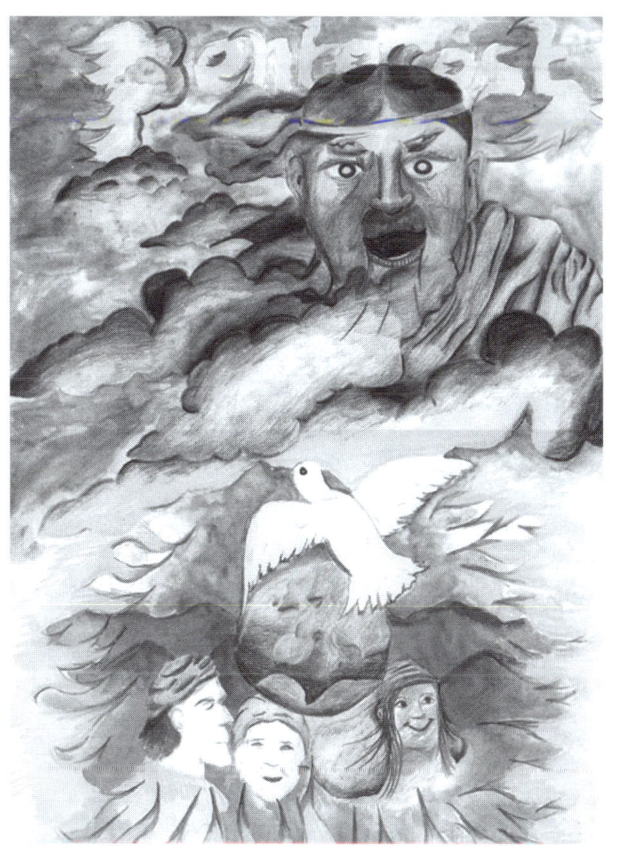

4. Planning many details in one image

This strategy asks pupils to take note of the scenes in a story and plan one image that retells the story (level 2) and makes links between its different elements (level 3). Use Picture card 6, the collage of the Buddha's 'Four Sights' by Farah, to exemplify this for children.

Take a story of faith you want to teach, and ask pupils to work on the story by imagining the key moment in the story for the central character. They should use a 'thought bubble sheet' to picture all the things the main character might have thought about around that key moment. For example, if the story was the birth of Jesus, and the key character Mary, the key moment might be as she cradles the infant Jesus. Her thoughts might be about the stable, the angel, the journey to Bethlehem and what will happen next. Ask pupils to analyse the story simply like this, and then to plan and make a collage of thoughtful images.

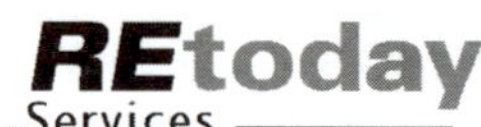

Looking at pictures with pupils in RE

Pictures can be used as a 'way in' to all sorts of RE topics and concepts, with all age-groups. The questions below help pupils to look closely at pictures and to engage imaginatively with them, deepening their understanding of both the art form and the subject matter. They encourage pupils to look at colour, pattern and texture, line and tone, shape, form and space to see how these are combined and used for different purposes. This activity can be used with any of the pictures in this *Spirited Arts* pack.

- Introduce a picture. Try using pictures which illustrate a faith story, or an ethical theme, or portraits of people experiencing different emotions, landscapes of different countries or cityscapes, fantasy pictures, abstract pictures – the possibilities are endless. Enlarge, cut up and give out an appropriate selection of the cards below. Pupils discuss their responses together in groups as a way of exploring the picture.
- Pupils could then pick the ten questions which they feel would be most important if they were going to help a younger pupil to explore the picture, or they could pick ten questions that 'appeal' to them personally or in pairs.
- Enlarge the diagram on the next page to A3. Fill the central box with small copies of the picture or ask pupils to sketch it. Pupils arrange the questions on the spiral in the order in which they want them to be considered.

These questions will help pupils to look really carefully at the paintings:	**These questions will help pupils to engage imaginatively with the paintings:**
How many different colours can you see/how many different shades of the same colour can you see?	What feelings do the colours and shades give you/how does this picture make you feel? What has the artist done to make you feel like that?
Are the colours bright or pale? Are they contrasting or blended? What effect does this have?	How do you think the artist was feeling when he/she painted this picture? How can you tell?
Are there any people or animals, flowers or other objects? How are they arranged?	What sort of thoughts and feelings does the artist want people to have when they look at this painting?
Are the lines in this painting straight or curved? Why?	If you could eat this painting, what sort of flavour would it have?
How many different shapes can you see? Does one shape stand out or are the shapes interlinked?	If you could listen to this painting, what sort of sound would it make?
How has the artist used light, shade and texture to create an effect?	If this picture was made from other materials, what would it be made of? What would it feel like to touch?
What sort of things might the artist have used (e.g. watercolour, oils or large or small brushes)? What effect has this had?	If this painting could talk, what might it say?
Do you think the work was done quickly or slowly? In one go or returned to many times? Why?	Would you like to have this picture on your wall at home, and why/why not?
What thoughts must this artist have had in order to create this picture?	Do you like the whole picture, or just parts of it? Why?
How old is this picture?	What can you say, by looking at this picture, about the artist? For example, are they young or old?
What do you think this picture is about?	What do you think this artist might believe?
A different question I would like to ask is…	If you could follow the artist around in secret for a day and a night, what might they be doing?

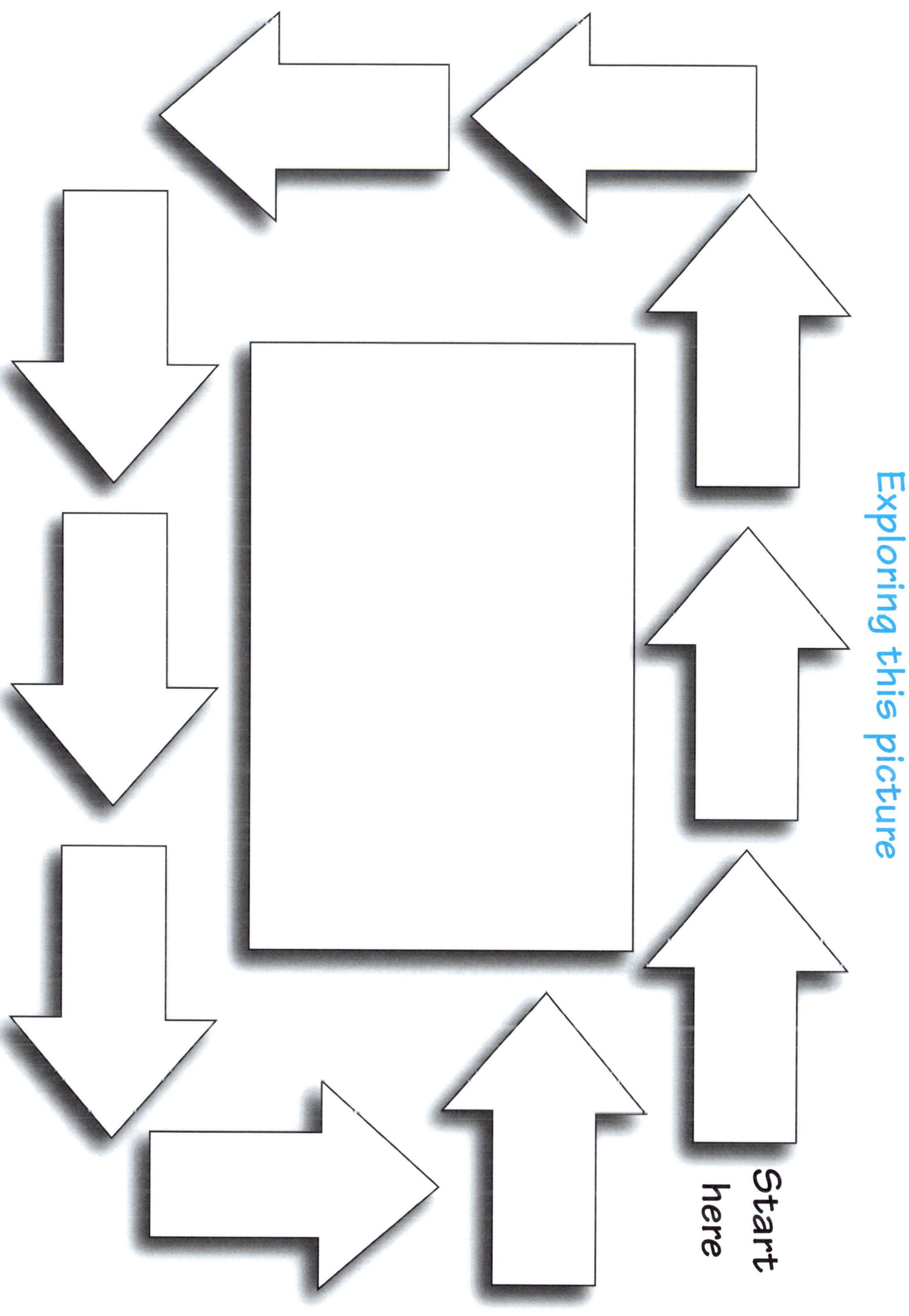
Exploring this picture
Start here

 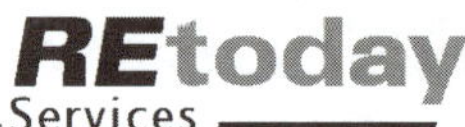

Gallery activities

Ideas to try when using art in RE or creating art in RE

Observing, questioning, concluding

- Talk about pupils' own perceptions about what they can see in the painting, what questions they would like to ask about it, and what meaning it holds for them.
- What can we say about the people in the picture, just by looking at and describing them? (For example, their clothes, expressions, body language.)
- The National Gallery's website has a feature called 'zoomables'. Provide a large magnifying glass and let pupils 'zoom in' on their favourite part of the painting. Can they explain why they like this part? Why is it important in the picture? What message or meaning does this 'zoomable' have? (See also page 3: observation frames).

These are good strategies to try with reference to these pictures in the Spirited Arts *pack: 2, 3, 5.*

Story and symbol

- Talk about a painting which depicts a point in a story from a faith tradition. Pupils could make a large classroom frieze which tells the story as a sequence rather than as a moment.
- Pupils could select a key moment from a story to depict in their own artwork. This moment could set in a different time or culture (see www.jesusmafa.com for examples of artwork depicting scenes from the life of Jesus set in Cameroon).
- Pupils could create a key character for the story using a selection of objects as symbols.

These are good strategies to try with reference to these pictures in the Spirited Arts *pack: 1, 2, 4a, 4b, 6.*

Memory and meaning

- Cover a picture with 'jigsaw pieces' – uncover and then re-cover each piece at random. Can pupils guess what this is a picture of? Repeat, asking them to try to remember and piece together the evidence to describe or identify the topic. Other 'jigsaw' strategies include cutting a print of a painting into jigsaw shapes for younger pupils to put together, and using suitable software.
- Maps from Memory: pupils work in groups to recreate a picture using 10-second exposures to the picture at a time. When each group has had a turn, the teacher gives some input: e.g. 'What is it a picture of?' 'How did you work together?' Hear what different groups did (perhaps broke the picture into sections – each person looking only at one section etc). Repeat the activity. Did they change the way they worked the second time around – why? Which methods of working seemed most effective?
- Pupils could play 'I spy' type memory games with a painting. Lucy Micklethwaite's books *I Spy – An Alphabet in Art* and *I Spy – Animals in Art* are good resources (see Resources list for details). Can pupils create their own memory game to help each other to remember the details of a picture as a way of explaining its meaning?

These are good strategies to try with reference to these pictures in the Spirited Arts *pack: 5, 6 and 8b.*

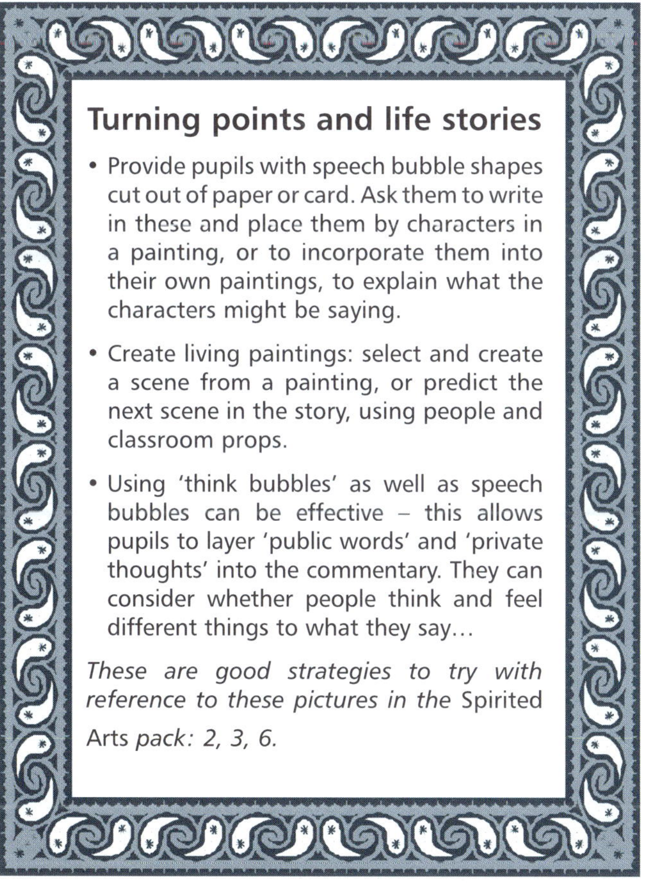

Turning points and life stories

- Provide pupils with speech bubble shapes cut out of paper or card. Ask them to write in these and place them by characters in a painting, or to incorporate them into their own paintings, to explain what the characters might be saying.
- Create living paintings: select and create a scene from a painting, or predict the next scene in the story, using people and classroom props.
- Using 'think bubbles' as well as speech bubbles can be effective – this allows pupils to layer 'public words' and 'private thoughts' into the commentary. They can consider whether people think and feel different things to what they say…

These are good strategies to try with reference to these pictures in the Spirited Arts *pack: 2, 3, 6.*

Creative expression

- Pupils could develop collages using only natural materials/synthetic materials/recyclable materials.
- Pupils could recreate a religious painting in a different format: e.g. collage, mosaic, 'stained glass', clay, sculpture, watercolour, cartoon.
- Pupils could draw self-portraits of the inside, rather than the outside, using symbols or symbolic colours and textures to express and represent different parts of their personalities and beliefs/ world view. How will they choose to record their feelings, thoughts, beliefs, personality, or 'spirit'?

These are good strategies to try with reference to all of the pictures in the Spirited Arts *pack.*

Strategies for using sculpture

- Use a blindfold or a feely bag to isolate the sense of touch, then ask pupils about the importance of touch in learning, and in expressing ourselves. 3D objects ask to be touched.
- Give pupils play dough, plasticine or clay to make their own mini-sculptures on a theme: hope, rainbow, feeling sorry, God's presence, and so on. A class can also create play dough scenes – e.g. everyone contributes one model to the 'Entry into Jerusalem' to make a crowd for digital photos.
- Using the same techniques and materials, pupils could try making faces of key emotions to illustrate a story, showing understanding of what people feel at key points.

These are good strategies to try with reference to these pictures in the Spirited Arts *pack: 8a, 8b.*

More strategies for using the prints in the 'Spirited Arts' pack

- 'Put yourself in the picture': Give each pupil a tiny post-it note, and ask them to draw their face on it. Take a picture that retells a story, then ask them to imagine they are 'in the scene'. Ask pupils to stick their post-it in some part of the picture. What could they see, hear and touch? What could the person nearest them be thinking? Imagine what they'd say to that person, and their reply. What are they going to do next? (Or ask other questions appropriate to the picture.) This works very well at developing empathic engagement, and drawing pupils into the story. Then move on to text work…
- Images and texts: Find a scriptural text (this could be from any religious tradition) that illuminates the work of art and ask: what does the image tell you about the words? How do the words help you understand the image?

 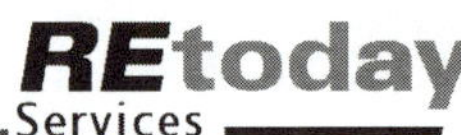

Using art in RE: painting

The parable of the Prodigal Son – Luke 15:11-32

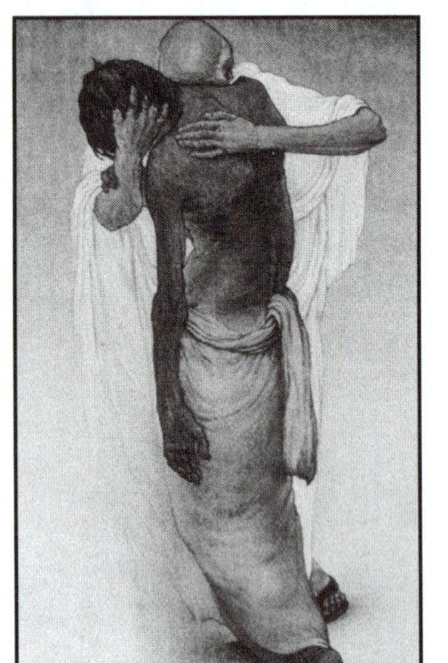

Parable: a story drawing on 'everyday' experiences to express key spiritual ideas and concepts.

Key Christian themes: Unconditional love – of the father for the son, of God for those who turn (return). The power of reconciliation and forgiveness – to restore broken relationship (with family, God and humanity). The importance of belonging (to the human and the Christian family).

To the left: an artist's impression of the key moment in this parable, by Frank Wesley – see full-colour version: http://dlibrary.acu.edu.au/research/theology/ejournal/aejt_4/farrell.htm. It can also be found in *Picturing Jesus pack B* by Lat Blaylock (RE Today 2004, ISBN 1-904024-44-0) and on the back cover of this publication.

Activity One: Considering feelings

Ask pupils, to look closely at the painting (about 1 minute) without talking. What do they see? What do they think is happening? Turn to a partner and share ideas. Feed back what three or four pairs think. Divide the class into two parts. Ask one half to think about the man whose back is facing us, and the other to think about the other man. Ask them to look at the painting again, without talking (about 1 minute), thinking about how their 'man' is feeling and why they think he is feeling that way. Turn to a partner who has been thinking about the other man's feelings, and share ideas. Take feedback from three or four pairs.

Retell the parable, asking pupils to think about how each of the characters might be feeling as the story progresses. Talk about how each character might have felt at different points in the story. (You could also plot a 'feelings graph' for each.) Have pupils ever had similar feelings? Frank Wesley thought the key moment in the story was the one he painted. Ask pupils if they would have chosen that same moment or a different one, and why. Give each pupil cut-outs of a speech bubble, a thought bubble and a feelings bubble (this could be heart-shaped). In the light of what they have thought about during the lesson, ask pupils to write on the shapes what both the father and the son might have said, thought and felt at their chosen moment. They can then stick them in their RE books as a record of their learning in this lesson.

About the artist and the painting

Frank Wesley (1923–2002): was born in Lucknow, India. He was a Christian (Methodist background). He was honoured to be chosen to design the urn that carried the ashes of Mahatma Gandhi before their release into the River Ganga (Ganges). Many of his works are based on biblical stories but he said that he was not interested in only illustrating them. He said an illustration was a depiction of a scene that could be 'observed with detachment'. He wanted his art to engage those who saw it with the key themes and ideas, the 'truths' the story was meant to convey.

'The Forgiving Father' was painted in 1989, based on the parable of the Prodigal Son. The moment chosen is when the son returns and is met by the father. **Contrasts:** for example, the Father (older) holding up the son (younger) as he falls into his arms. Father: loving embrace – son: dejection and despair. Father: rich, well-fed, clean clothing (Brahmin – high-caste) – son: thin, dishevelled and in dirty clothing (Dalit – 'untouchable'). The artist uses pink to convey the divine – it is there in the background and in the robe of the father, and it is seeping into the son's cloth. We cannot see faces, but as the viewer we are next in line to be greeted by the father…

Activity Two: Under the magnifying glass – zoom image facility

Divide pupils into pairs or threes and give each group a magnifying glass to look very carefully at the painting, focusing on colour, shape and texture. Ask them to select one part of the painting (e.g. the younger son's hand hanging down or the father's hand cradling his son's head) to 'zoom in on'. How does the artist depict the emotions of the story?

The National Gallery website, in its education section (www.nationalgallery.org.uk/education/visits/resources.htm) has a collection of paintings with a 'zoom image' facility. A number of these are depictions of different parts of the Christmas (and Easter) stories: for example, 'Mystic Nativity' by Botticelli (1500), 'The Holy Family with a Shepherd' by Titian (circa 1510), 'The Adoration of the Kings' by Veronese (1573). This facility allows pupils to select a specific part of the painting (favourite, most interesting, most colourful, most puzzling, or whatever) for closer scrutiny. It encourages close observation and, if pupils are effectively prompted, it can support questioning (of the artist, the painting, the story), speculation (the artist's motivation, the purpose of the story) and coming to conclusions (about the meaning and interpretation of the painting/story). Asking how the artist created feeling and mood by the use of colour, texture, brush stroke, light and shade helps to focus attention. Other questions might relate to why the artist chose to paint this part of the story, and in this way; what 'message' the artist was trying to 'put across' and why; whether it is a 'true' reflection of the story in the Bible (or other faith source). For example, Christians believe that Jesus is a very special baby – how does the 'Mystic Nativity' show that belief?

You can use this approach on a wide range of images, using either computers for individual or small group work or an interactive whiteboard for whole class use.

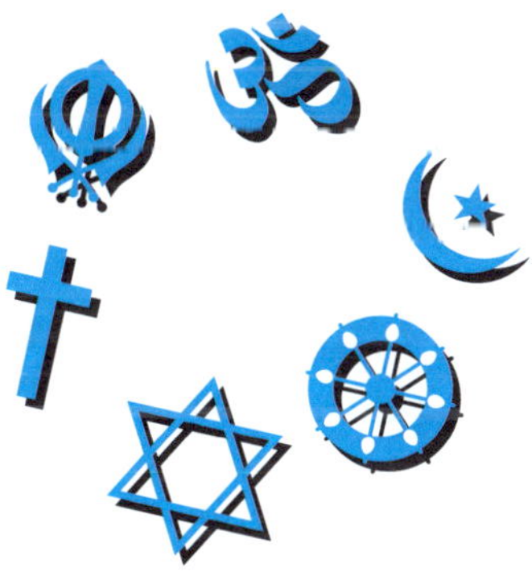

Activity Three: Freeze-frame (human sculpture) of a turning point

Take a look at Emily's work on 'The Lost Sheep' and Farah's on 'The Four Sights of the Buddha' for examples of artwork produced on the theme of 'turning points'. Craig and Derya's pictures capture a key moment in the Islamic story of Muhammad (PBUH) and the Angel Jibril, following Islamic rules about not depicting living forms. Talk about how each of these picture cards conveys the turning point of the story.

As a demonstration, ask two volunteers to become a sculpture of 'The Forgiving Father' painted by Wesley. They are to stand still and be pliable, allowing others to sculpt them rather than doing it themselves. Stand them in a prominent position in the classroom, preferably in front of a white sheet so that the background does not distract. Ask two other volunteers to 'be the sculptors', looking carefully at the painting and placing the 'characters' in position.

Ask pupils in groups of 4 to focus on a different parable e.g. the Good Samaritan (Luke chapter 10 verses 29–37) – and decide what is the turning point of the story and why (most will choose the Samaritan stopping to help the man, bandaging him, lifting him onto the donkey). Encourage them to talk in their groups about what the characters would be thinking/feeling and what they might have said to each other. Then prepare the freeze-frame or human sculpture as above with two people 'sculpting' and two being the 'models'. After their sculpting and whilst they are still in position, the teacher will touch each figure on the shoulder – that is the signal for the character to share, in role, what they are thinking or feeling at that moment in time.

Take a digital picture of each group's freeze-frame. Compare these with other pictures of the story of the Good Samaritan that you can find. For two examples in very different styles see:

www.asianchristianart.org/profile/HeQi/pages/TheGoodSamaritan.htm

www.metmuseum.org/Works_Of_Art/viewOnezoom.asp?dep=11&zoomFlag=0&viewmode=1&item=30%2E31

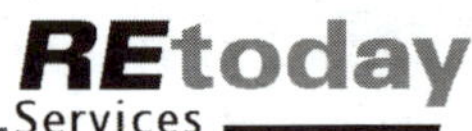

Using art in RE: sculpture

A sculpture invites the viewer to look at it from different angles, to touch and to feel, to become physically and often spiritually involved with it. Religious themes have been a favourite subject for sculptors throughout history and continue to be a source of inspiration for many today.

The activities here help pupils to engage with sculpture and to respond sensitively to the religious concepts and teaching behind the artist's work. They then use these as a springboard for their own creativity and expression, using the medium of sculpture to show their understanding and to make links between their own ideas and the religious concepts encountered.

Activity One: Exploring symbolism in sculpture, using picture cards 8a and 8b by Jess and Chloe

- Fix each picture card in the centre of a large piece of card or paper.
- In groups, pupils come out and look carefully at the sculptures for one minute.
- Pupils talk in their groups about the various features of the sculptures (e.g. the yellow circle, the hands, the word 'love', the dove, the cross). On speech bubbles they describe what these features might mean. Each group places their speech bubbles around the picture. (For younger pupils, make cards with images and words which they can match, e.g. yellow ring = sun.) Talk about the different ideas. Make the point that sculptors often use symbols to put across a message or meaning.
- Then read what Jess and Chloe said about their sculptures and talk about the symbols and their intended meanings.
- Give each pupil a new speech bubble. Ask them to retell the message of one of the sculptures in their own words. Display all the speech bubbles with the picture cards.

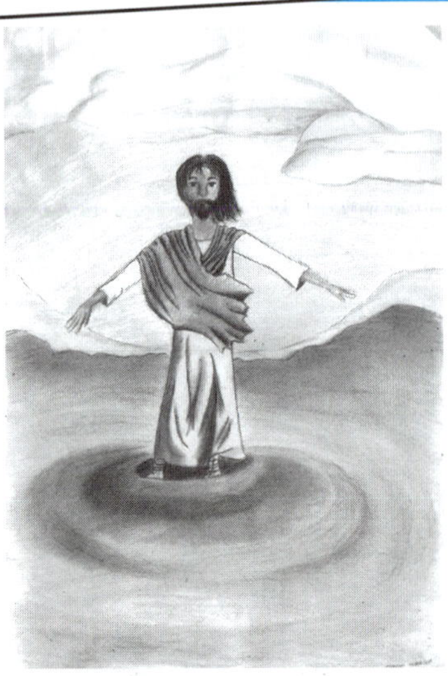

Activity Two: Living sculptures

In this activity lower primary pupils can encounter the beliefs and teachings of a religious faith through a sacred story. This is used as the inspiration for creating 'living sculptures' in the classroom. The example here uses 'Jesus calms the storm' (Luke 8:22–25). Pupils work in groups.

- Read the story and talk about what it means. Discuss how the disciples might have felt. How might Jesus have felt?
- Each group selects one scene from the story to 'freeze-frame', and rehearses this, remembering to use facial expression and body language to make their point clear. Guide pupils in their choice by asking them to consider:
  - What does this story tell us about Jesus?
  - What do you want your 'frozen moment' to say to an onlooker?
- Digitally photograph each group's 'frozen moment' from a number of angles.
- Using the digital photographs to help them, pupils create a sculpture of their moment. Provide a range of materials, including synthetic and natural objects as well as clay, plasticine, card, wood, empty containers, glue, sticky tape. Modroc and chicken wire are messy but particularly effective.
- Talk about how the living sculptures retell the story and describe its meaning.

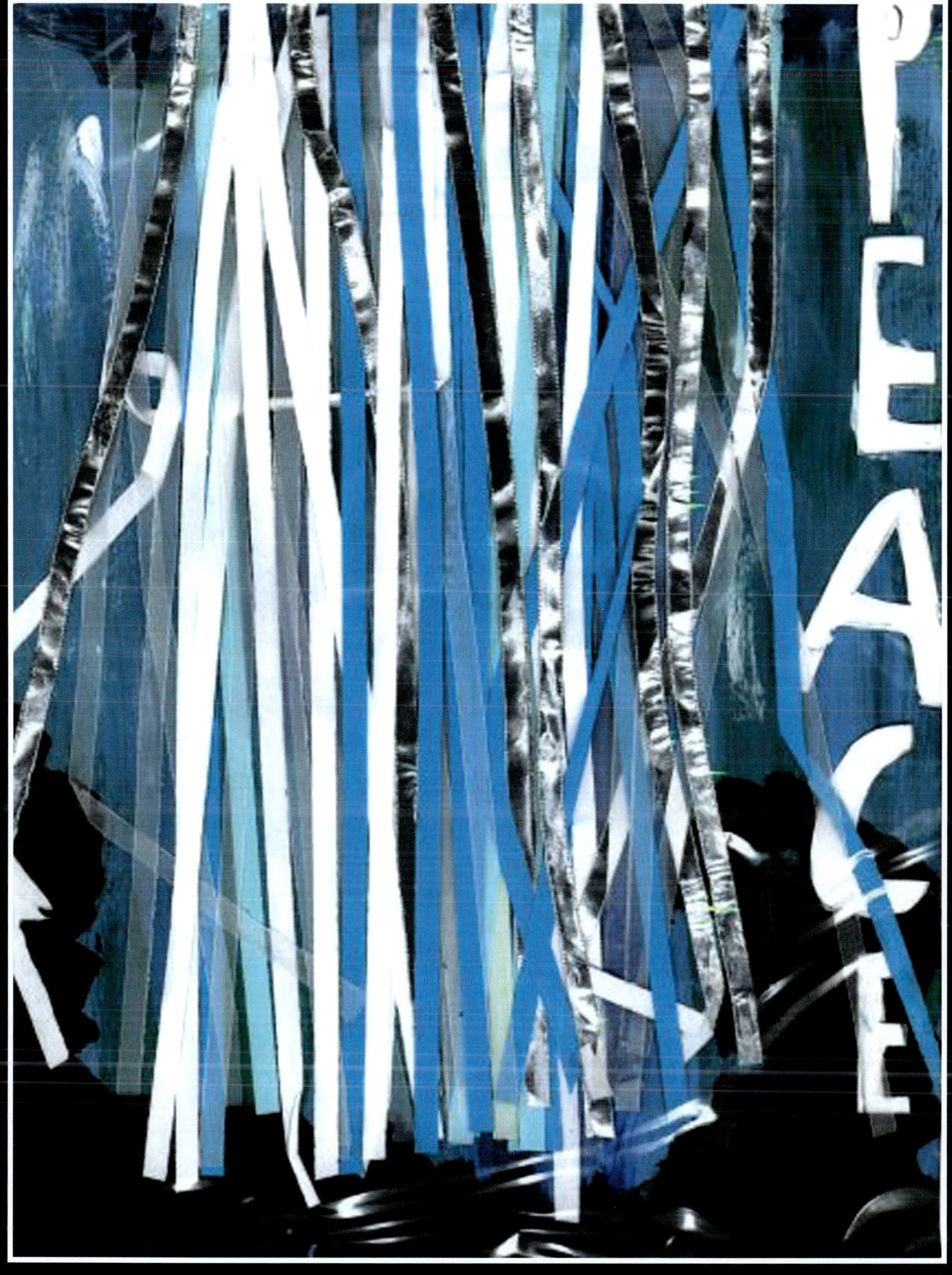

Picture Card 1
Rory, age 7

Rory said:

Peace: I love waterfalls. They are peaceful places to me. I like the water in the sunlight when it shines like a rainbow and like snow.

The Spirited Arts judges said:

Rory has created a beautiful image of peace, linked to the world of nature (as so many of our ideas about peace often are). The ribboning of foil, paper and cloth creates the remarkably good feeling of 'water falling' He's able to link the idea of inner peace to the outer world – this is a spiritual piece of work for this reason.

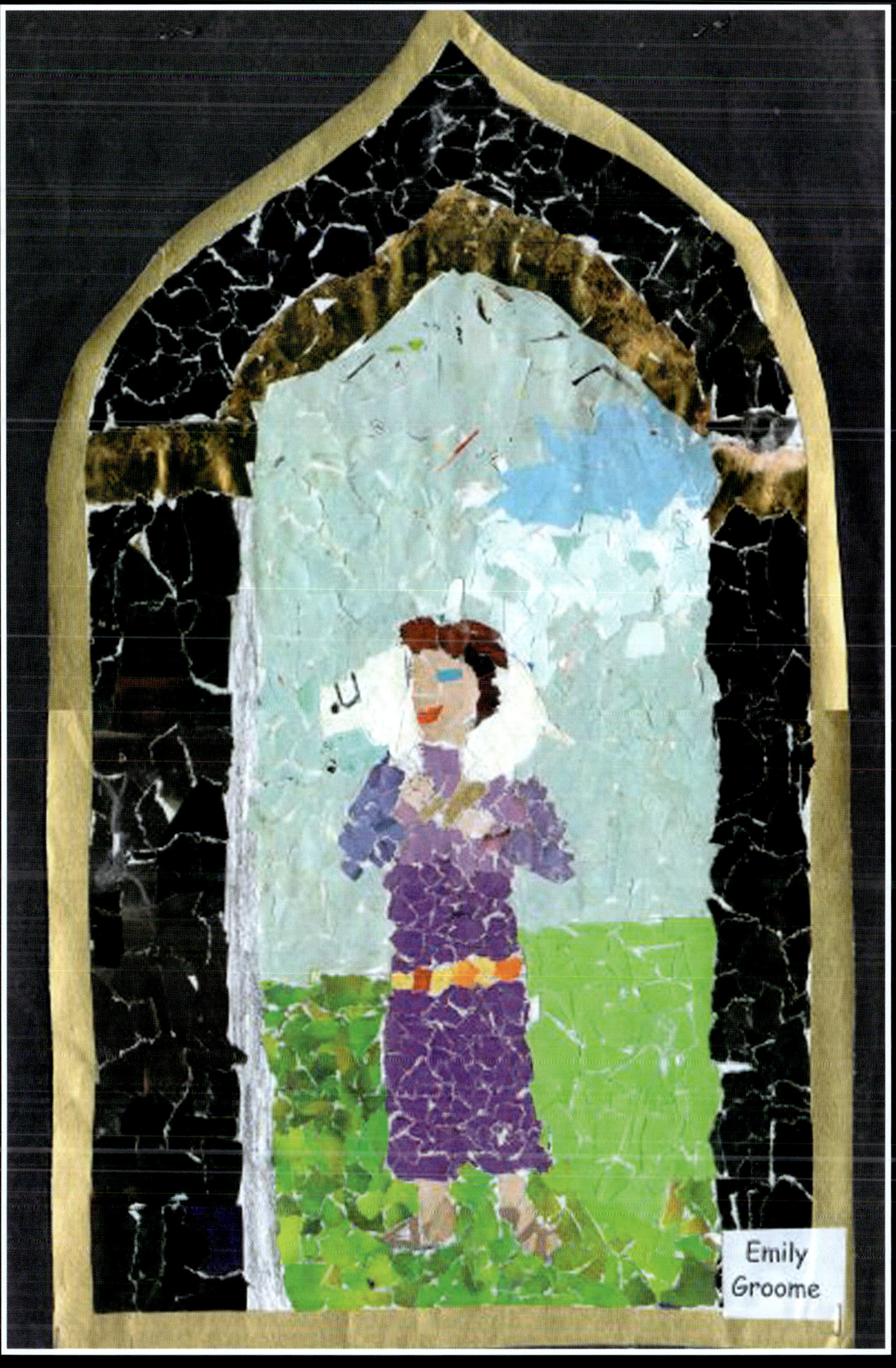

Picture Card 2
Emily, age 8

Emily said:

The lost sheep – I've brought him home. I knew this story very well from my literacy and RE lessons. My picture shows the Good Shepherd bringing home the lost sheep. It's a turning point for the story because now the Sheep is safe and free from danger. I've made a collage from torn paper. We had been talking about the custom of well dressings that are a tradition in Derbyshire where I live. I decided to make a collage to represent the well dressing, using torn paper instead of flower petals. It's a good picture to make anyone feel safe.

The Spirited Arts judges said:

Emily's work is local because she picks up the Derbyshire tradition of well dressing in her tissue-collage, and is biblical – it identifies the turning point of the Parable of the Lost Sheep. We found the care and attention to both text and image an inspiring example of the depth of what an 8-year-old can achieve.

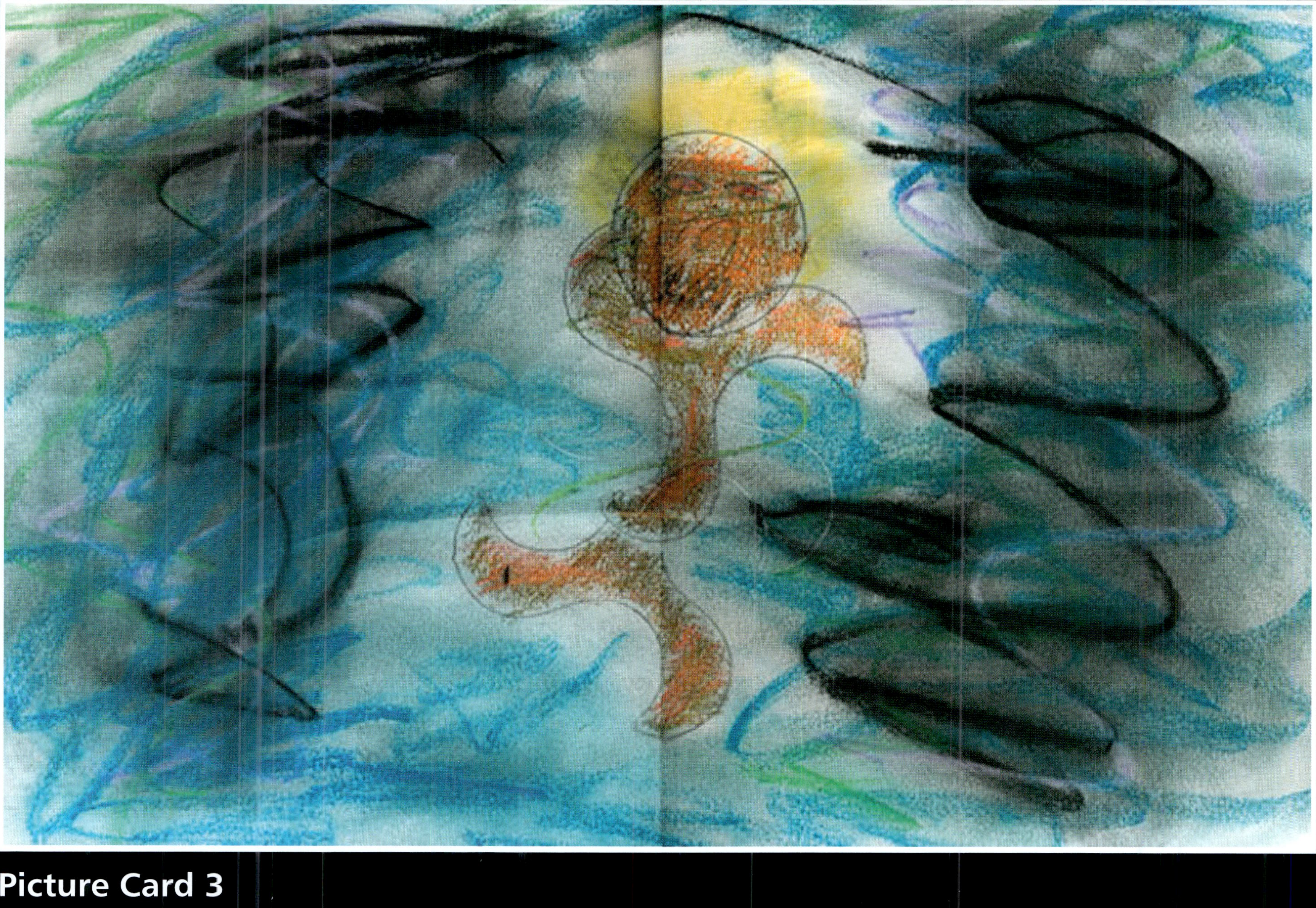

Picture Card 3
Curtis, age 8

Curtis said:

This is what I think my spirit looks like. I chose reds, oranges and yellows because I get angry very easily. I chose my shapes because I am always running about and I am always nuts at home. This is *my spirit.*

The Spirited Arts judges said:

Many teachers feel wary of approaching the topic of spirituality with younger pupils, but this teacher used a saying of Jesus ('Father, into your hands I commit my spirit') to examine the idea with pupils in Y3. From this beginning, Curtis has been able to think about how his own spirit can be represented in an image, and to create the image. It's vibrant, expressive and accurate.

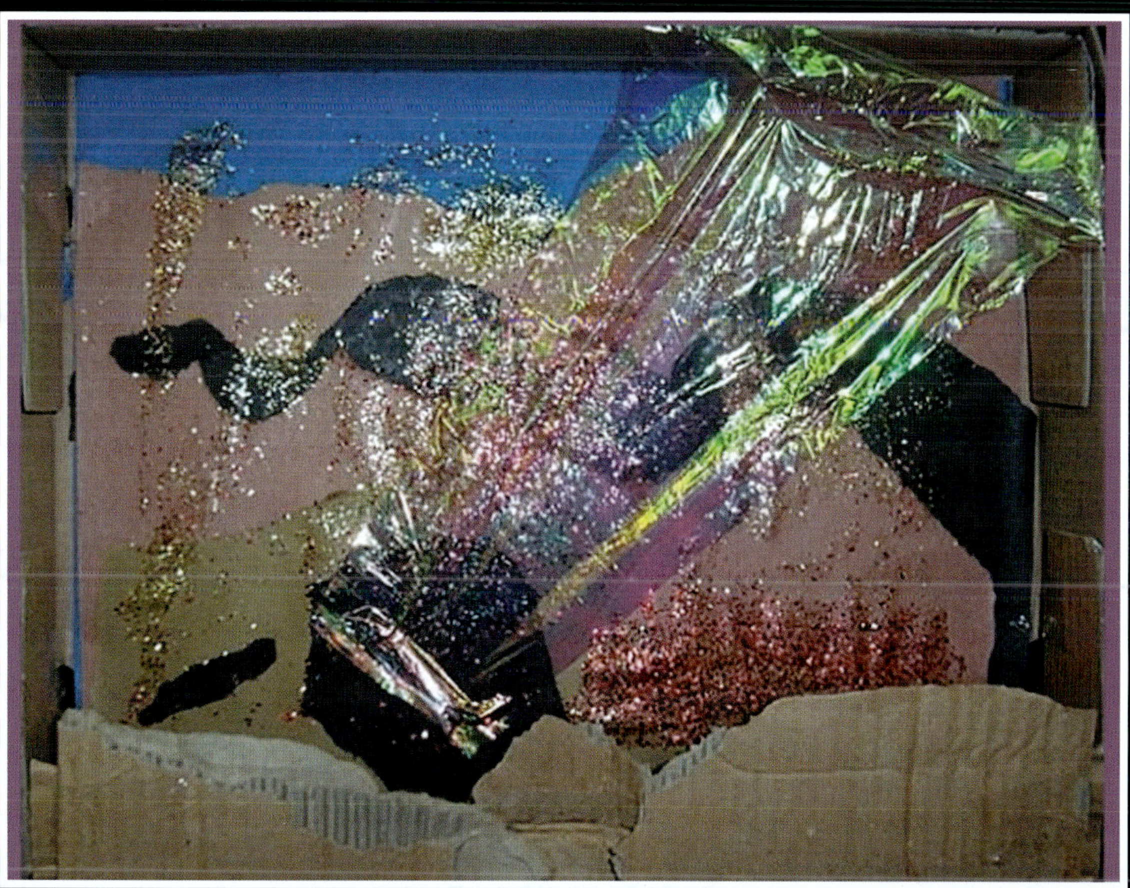

Picture 4a
Craig, age 14

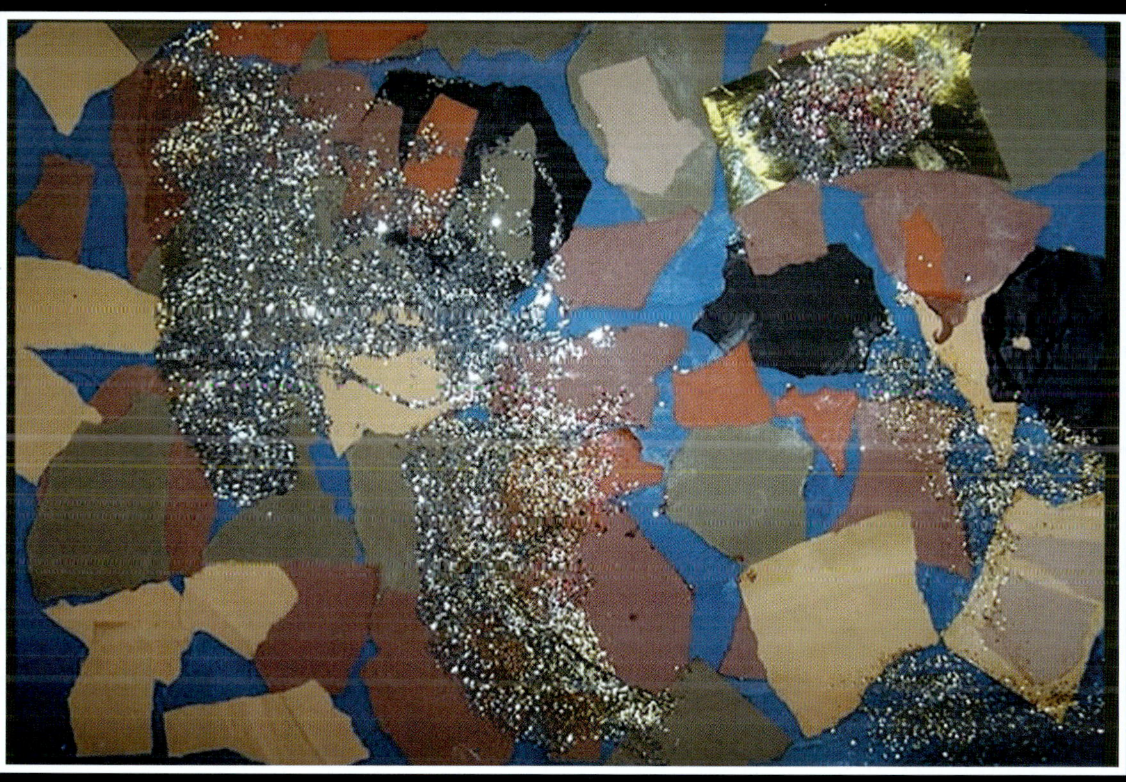

Picture 4b
Derya, age 14

Craig said:

Heavenly Light: This pupil is an atheist who has questioned the existence of God. He finds writing extremely difficult yet was inspired to write after September 11, 'Why do bad things happen to good people?' Here the iridescent cellophane is used as a veil to show light bonding the cave to heaven. He also produced a long panel with a friend, showing the transition after Mohammed (pbuh) met the angel, with bright red disturbing colours changing to peaceful and beautiful clouds.

Derya said:

God is in the Gold: This is the first piece of work we have ever seen this pupil complete independently. Her support teachers were stunned and delighted by her commitment to the task. A Turkish Muslim, she describes her most special things as 'Turkish'. She shows love to everyone she meets. When she heard the recitation she began to pray. She was insistent that God was the gold area in the picture.

These pieces come from a selection of work achieved by children with a range of difficulties including autism, speech and communication difficulties, behavioural difficulties, dyslexia, cerebral palsy and Downs' syndrome. Some are among the least able children in their school. Their inspiration was the Muslim story of Mohammed (pbuh) and the Angel Jibril.

The Spirited Arts judges said:

These images use Islamic rules for imagery, and explore the idea of an angelic message with real insight and sensitivity. They focus on the deeper meaning of Islamic story, and show the truth that sometimes pupils with special needs also have special insights and express themselves with special skill.

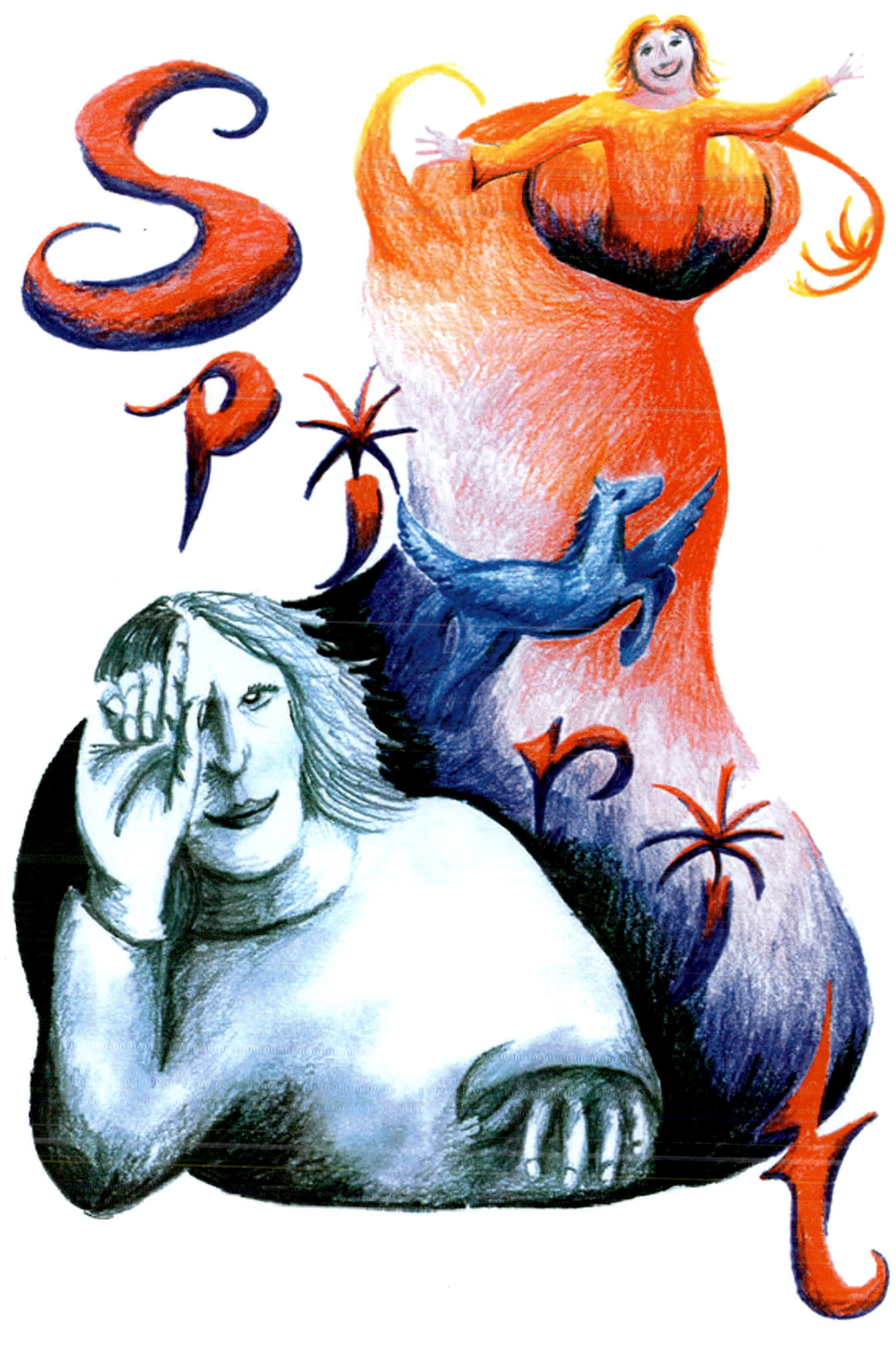

Picture 5

Kate said:

Through this poster I tried to portray that sometimes day to day life can hide the true person within. We can seem withdrawn and are often shy to express our feelings, because we get wrapped up in work and this causes stress and often unhappiness. Therefore in this poster I've depicted the greyness of the exterior of the person, coming to life and revealing the colourful, dramatic, powerful soul and spirit within. Remember never judge a book by its cover; always look within, for its true meaning.

Someone's spirit is special but is even more special if it's shown and shared.

The Spirited Arts judges said:

Kate's image speaks volumes about how our society can lock out or suppress the spiritual. She sees children as the lively winged horse or the girl escaping from a black hole into light. But we often see them as grey, shy or quiet. Kate's image is spiritually vibrant, from her own experience and generalised into a challenging piece of art.

A suffering person
(suffering)
An old man (old)
A holy man, who is happy
and content, for he has
helped someone.
RIP
The Dead (Death)

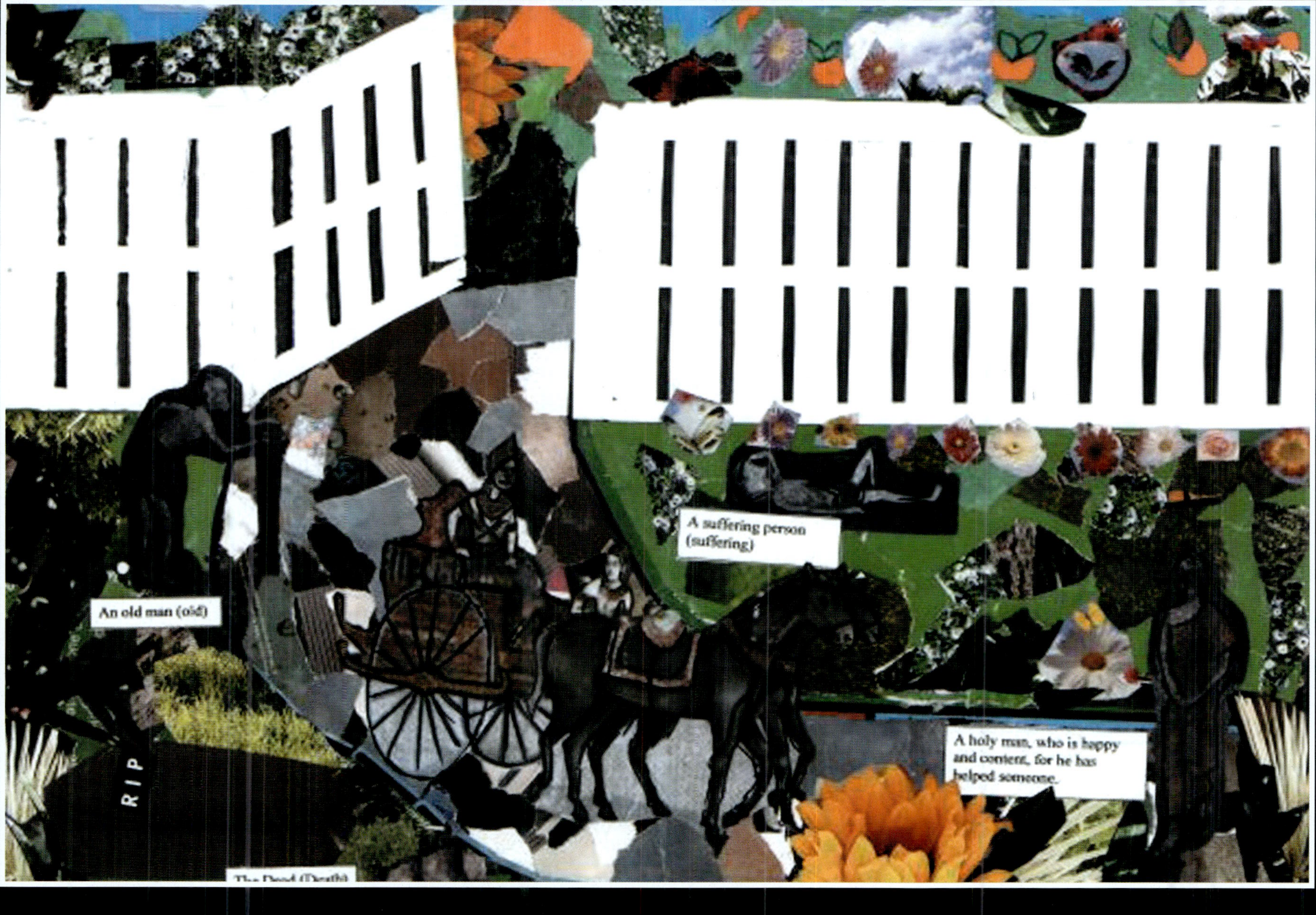

Picture 6

Farah said:

To create this piece of art I made a collage. This shows the turning point when Siddhartha Gautama left his palace to see the world beyond it. He hadn't seen suffering, death or old age before, and this picture shows the moment when he first does. Siddhartha also sees a holy man, happy and content for he had helped others. When Siddhartha was born, his father asked what would become of him. Wise men said he would be a great man. They also told him that if the boy saw suffering he would be a religious leader rather than a great ruler. Because of this his father did not allow anyone sick or old to come near him. That's the reason this is the turning point of his story. He did become a religious leader, who we all know today as the Buddha.

The Spirited Arts judges said:

This piece reflects profound engagement with the stories of the Buddha, and makes space for genuine reflection on the meaning of these stories for anyone – it shows what learning from Buddha might mean. The detail and accuracy are great, but it's the allusiveness of the collage that really makes it worth looking at for a long time. Farah's text identifies the 'turning point ' of the story, and as such is an insightful interpretation of a Buddhist narrative.

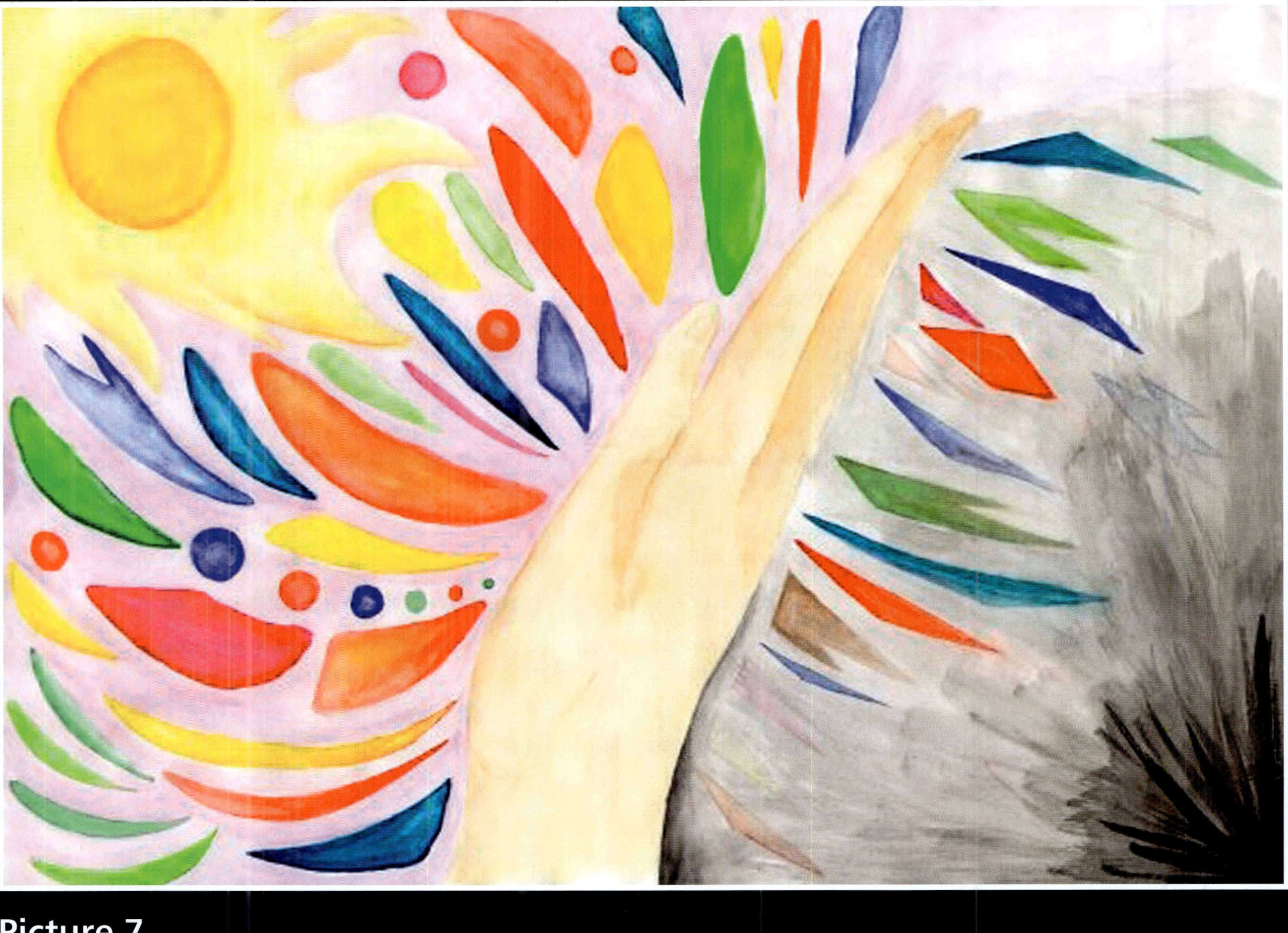

Picture 7

Holly said:

My soul painting depicts a hand stopping aspects of my personality getting through which is how I feel sometimes.

Sometimes it feels like I have to stop saying some of the things I do and that I have to hold back what I really think or feel about certain things.

So, in a way, the hand represents public opinion or morals.

The darkness on the right is to show that the aspects of my personality on that side aren't shown often. The ones on the left are the ones I show often - they are in the light.

There is a space in the top right hand corner where the personalities mix so it shows that sometimes you cannot hold back emotion.

The Spirited Arts judges said:

As a reflection on the meaning of one's own spirit, Holly's work is remarkable. Full of insight and self-awareness, she images the spirit without reference to religion, but clearly addresses through her planned work issues of identity, community, virtue and psychology. Good art raises questions for the viewer, and a long look at this can't help but make you ask: 'How would I picture my spiritual life?'

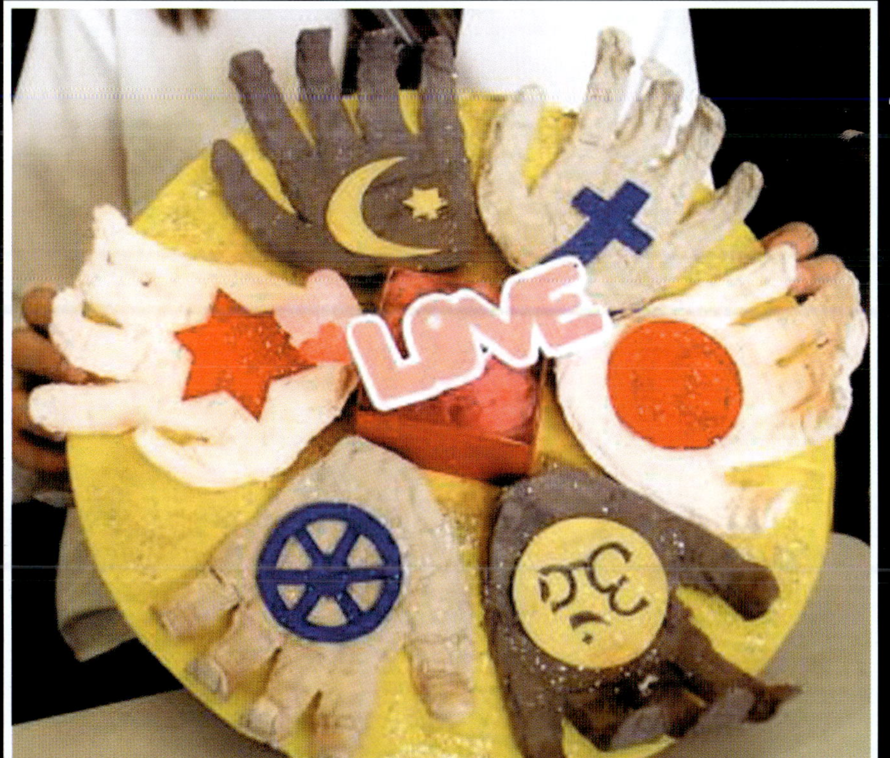

Picture 8a
Jess, age 13

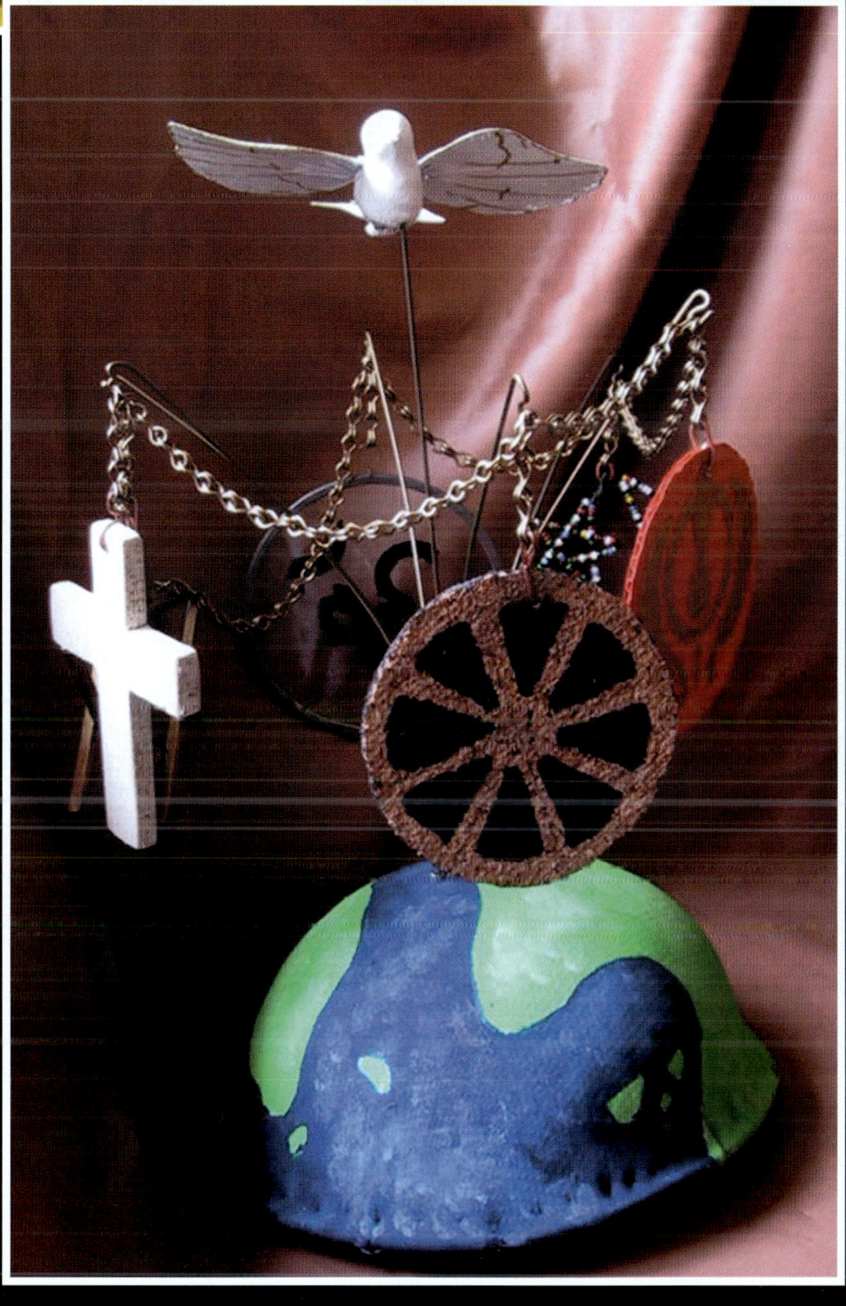

Picture 8b
Chloe, age 14

Jess said:
The small red box in the centre symbolises the love in our world through every religion and race. The circle, which the hands and the box are stuck onto, stands for the sunshine beaming down, making everybody happy and peaceful. The hands in which the symbols are held symbolise united races and religions. The religious symbols show that every religion in the world counts. My work means: no matter what colour or religion there should still be happiness, love and unity through the world. We are all equals.

The Spirited Arts judges said:
Many entries to Art in Heaven use the symbols of 6 religions, but this one is outstanding because of the well thought out arrangement and the juxtapositions of symbols that have meanings beyond the individual faiths. This is not syncretistic – each faith is clearly itself. But open hands, sunshine and the red box symbolise a vision or need for faiths to relate to each other as well as to assert themselves. It's both beautifully conceived and beautifully executed.

Chloe said:
Hopes for the future: The world's population is supported by many religions, all with the same basic principals. In my piece I have selected the main six, and they are represented by their symbols, which are made of six different materials: brass, wood, glass, beads, cork and painted cardboard. The symbols are linked with a chain to show that they are united together. There is a dove in the centre of the ring to represent peace between all people, whatever their race, culture or religion.

The Spirited Arts judges said:
Chloe's ideas about linking religions and about the pre-eminence of peace are clear from the image she has created, and her willingness to address inter faith issues and develop her ideas about the space between religions are coupled with her skilful 'design and make' work to produce this ultimately hopeful symbol of the world's religious futures.

'The Angel of the North'

by Antony Gormley

90,000 motorists a day and passengers travelling on the East Coast mainline pass 'The Angel of the North', making it one of the most viewed statues in the world, and the biggest. The angel is made of steel, shaped like a jumbo jet. It stands strong and powerful on top of a disused coal mine as a symbol of the region's regeneration, hope and strength.

'The angel has three functions – firstly a historic one to remind us that below this site coal miners worked in the dark for two hundred years, secondly to grasp hold of the future expressing our transition from the industrial to the information age, and lastly to be a focus for our hopes and fears.'

(Antony Gormley)

Questions to get pupils 'thinking and talking':

Use images at www.angelofthenorth.org.uk and www.kenfinn.demon.co.uk/angel/ in the classroom.

- Do you like or dislike the sculpture? Why?
- When you look at 'The Angel of the North' what do you think of?
- Why do you think Antony Gormley chose an angel for his sculpture?

Angels in sacred traditions

- The word 'angel' means 'messenger'.
- In the Bible, angels are servants and messengers of God, who are also sent to help and protect people. However, the Bible also mentions that not all angels are good. Luke1:11–19, Luke 1:26–38 and Matthew 28:1–7 tell stories of angels bringing messages from God.
- Jews and Christians are not alone in having angels mentioned in their sacred texts. Great importance is given to angels in Islam, where they are believed to be 'unseen' creatures who act in God's service as 'intermediaries' between God and humanity. Gabriel (Jibril) is the angel who revealed the Qur'an to the Prophet Muhammad (pbuh). According to Surah 50.18 in the Qur'an, everyone has two guardian angels who record the person's good and bad deeds.
- Ask pupils to imagine an angel bringing a message from God today. What might the angel say and who might the message be for: themselves? Your school? The world's leaders? Someone else?

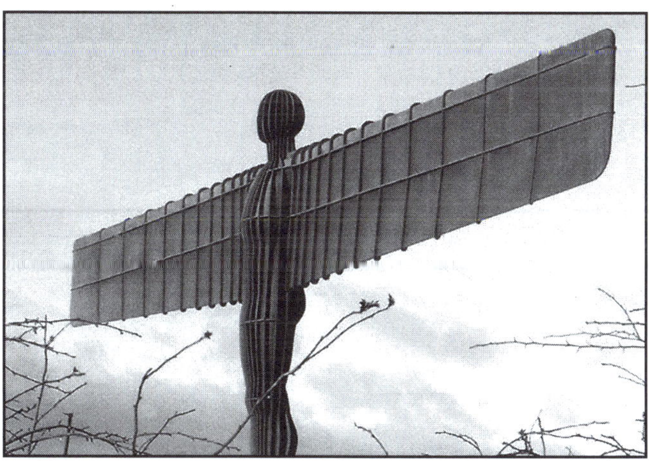

Activity Three: Creating a sculpture to explore a concept

- Upper primary pupils could create a sculpture to show their understanding of the concept of 'angel': either one with moving parts, one made from found objects, a synthetic sculpture or a natural sculpture.
- Provide something from each of these categories for pupils to work with to turn into a sculpture: e.g. a coat hanger, a branch, an empty washing-up liquid bottle, an orange. Ask pupils to choose an object and handle it, exploring possibilities: Which way up could it go? What could be added to it to change the shape/texture/colour? What could it be used for? Let them explore their object and sketch possible designs.
- Provide materials for them to use as they transform their object into a sculpture: e.g. chicken wire, paint, newspapers and magazines, bin liners, toilet roll tubes, stones and pebbles, pieces of wood, foil, matchsticks, acorns and conkers, elastic bands, plasticine, empty coke cans, empty water bottles, modroc, coloured beads, paper clips, leaves, drawing pins, copper wire, feathers, sequins, glitter, candles, cling film, string, fabric, glue, sticky tape, scissors and craft equipment, and so on.
- They could transform their object in a number of ways: by squashing it, folding it or cutting it, gluing things to it, tying things to it, wrapping things round it, changing the colour, creating different textures.
- Pupils working at level 3 will be able to describe the message of their sculpture, making links with their religious learning. Those working at level 4 could suggest the meaning of their sculpture, applying their ideas and their learning on this topic. Where would they like their angel to be situated, and why?

 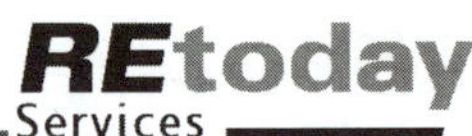

Using art in RE: Christian art

The image of the cross is central in Christianity, as a reminder of the last week of Jesus' life and of key beliefs about salvation, suffering, sacrifice and renewal. The cross has become a powerful decorative symbol, used in jewellery, churches, the environment and art to convey religious concepts or to make a social comment. It can comfort and it can challenge.

Work in this section looks at two different ways in which Christians use the cross as an art form: to remind people about key events in Jesus' life (Stations of the Cross in Roman Catholic churches) and to convey Christian beliefs about God and the world (Celtic crosses).

- Use Emily's picture from the pack, 'The Lost Sheep', as a stimulus. Talk about the 'cross shape' of the shepherd with the sheep across his shoulders, and the themes in the story which connect with Easter themes e.g. self-sacrifice, being saved, love and reconciliation.
- Look at some crosses with pupils and sort them into categories: is this cross beautiful or ugly? Is it simple or complicated? What colours, images and textures have been used? What is the artist saying to us through this cross? An online exhibition of decorative crosses can be found at www.ecva.org/exhibition/cross/pages/gallery.html Different crosses can be bought from artefact suppliers (see website addresses inside back cover, or from Christian bookshops.

Stations of the Cross

- Arrange a visit to a Roman Catholic church and focus on the Stations of the Cross. Ask your host to explain how worshippers use the Stations in prayer. An online meditation for children, with a Roman Catholic emphasis, can be seen at: www.cptryon.org/prayer/child/stations
- Talk to pupils about what each Station depicts.
- As part of a wider topic on Easter the Stations could be used to recall or exemplify key Easter events and Christian beliefs about Jesus, as appropriate for pupils' age and abilities. Pupils could look at how these images/sculptures might help Christians to remember and celebrate Holy Week. Talk about pupils' own reactions to the artwork. In some churches the Stations are very ornate and detailed; in others they are simple but evocative. What does the style and workmanship say about these Christians' feelings surrounding this story, their church, the way they express their beliefs?

Activities for pupils after the visit

- Learning about religion: pupils could work in groups to create a series of 14 Stations of the Cross, to go around the classroom. Give each group a different Station to design and create. Provide a variety of materials so that pupils can consider the style in which they would like to portray this part of Jesus' life and why they want to do it in this way. Look again at Emily's picture and find out about well dressing in Derbyshire in spring (e.g. www.peakleisure.co.uk/well_dressing_in_derbyshire). Could pupils re-create the Stations of the Cross in this style? Why might this appeal to a Christian? Pupils could write explanatory paragraphs to accompany their Stations.
- Learning from religion: pupils could consider how Jesus or the people he encountered might have been feeling at the particular moment they are illustrating, and how they will convey that in their art. They could talk about times in their own lives when they have felt like this.

Celtic crosses

Examples of Celtic crosses can be found through an internet image search.

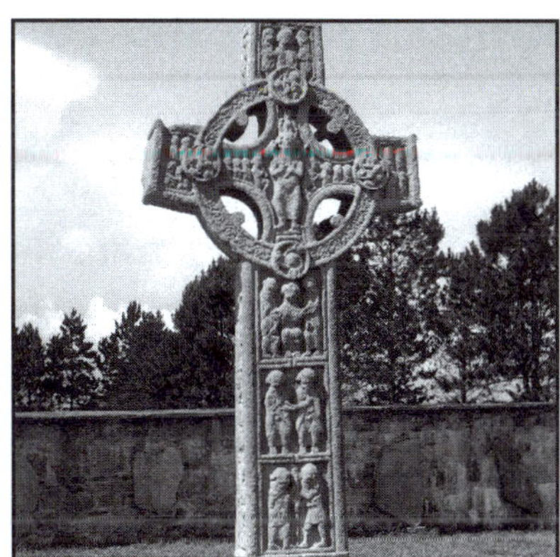

Celtic Christianity dates from a time when new Christian beliefs mingled with local pagan beliefs about the unity of creation, the sacredness of nature and the divine spark in all living things. Celtic crosses have a circle linking the four parts, representing the oneness of God, the sun which brings light and life, and the cycle of life and the seasons. The crosses are usually decorated with nature-based interlacing patterns symbolic of the importance and sacredness of the natural world, and a central boss representing either God or the sun as Jesus, light of the world.

Activity One: Sacred places

- Celtic crosses were often huge sculptures, marking sacred spaces. Lower primary pupils could recognise and name (level 1) places which are special to them – actual or emotional, here today or existing in memory – and talk about how they mark these places.
- Celtic Christians called sacred places 'thin' places – the divide between the human world and the world of God was thin enough to be broken through. Thin places include hilltops because people have a clear view from them; wells because people go down deep into the depths to discover fresh life-giving water; and bridges because they connect people to things they would otherwise be cut off from. Upper primary pupils could make links (level 3) between these ideas and their own experiences by identifying any symbolic hilltops (places or things which help them to see things clearly for what they really are), wells (places or things which help them find new strength), and bridges (places or things which connect or link them to other places, people, thoughts and feelings), in their own lives. Can they describe and draw their own symbolic landscape?

Activity Two: Symbolic shapes

- *Learning about religion:* There is plenty of scope here for pupils to design crosses with all sorts of features as an assessment task at the end of a topic on Christianity. Ask pupils to design a Celtic cross to express their understanding:
  - What do they think is the most central belief for Christians?
  - What could be the circle which links the different parts of Christianity?
  - What interlacing patterns could they decorate their cross with which might represent some important aspects of Christian belief or worship?
- *Learning from religion:* Pupils design a shape, which may be a cross but could be something else, which conveys their own beliefs and values. What will they put in the centre? What will link all the different parts? What will their symbolic decorations be? What are they symbolic of?

 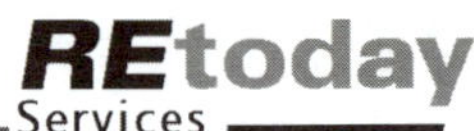

Creating artwork in RE: Buddhism

This creative strategy for learning about the life of the Buddha uses the traditional story, retold in 30 sentences. After getting to grips with the story, each pupil is given one sentence to illustrate. The 30 pictures produced can be bound together in order to create a memorable class book of the life of the Buddha.

Eight steps to making your class book

1. Copy the story from page 17 onto card, enlarging it to double the size. Make enough sets for there to be one between three or four pupils. Shuffle the pieces in each set and put them in an envelope.
2. Tell the story of the life of the Buddha, basing it around the 30 sentences on page 17. Make your retelling as vivid as you can – search for the 'Jackanory presenter within'!
3. Give a set of sentences to each group of 3 or 4 pupils. Ask them to re-assemble the story in the right order. This takes some time, and is complex – let them struggle to do it. They will interpret the story as they work.
4. Tell pupils about the class book. Show them the picture card of Farah's work on the four sights, and show them the picture here as well – a large colour version can be found at www.pcfre.org.uk/spiritedarts Talk about how these two young people have pictured the story they have been studying. If possible show them some other artistic representations of the story, from picture books, comic strips or other Buddhist art.
5. Allocate each child a single sentence to illustrate. Match these to pupils' learning needs. Some are simple (e.g. 1, 3, 9, 21); others are for the high achievers to be challenged, both conceptually and artistically (e.g. 5, 14, 22, 25). Ask them to discuss their part of the story in their group, giving each other suggestions. They could make a sketch of how they're going to approach the picture before starting on a final version.
6. Give pupils plenty of time and good materials to work with to make a picture that illustrates their part of the story. They should stick the sentence they're illustrating onto the page somewhere – or write it out. Spending time on this imaginative, creative, collective engagement with the central story of the Buddhist religion is worthwhile as RE – and can be good art education too.
7. When the pictures are all complete, arrange them as a gallery around the classroom walls. Invite a younger class to come and look, and ask your pupils to re-tell the story, using the pictures, for a group of smaller children.
8. Set a homework competition to design the cover for the book, and hold a class vote to choose a winner. Bind the 30 pages and the cover into the best-looking book you can. (Teachers may wish to keep this product as evidence of class attainments and achievements.)

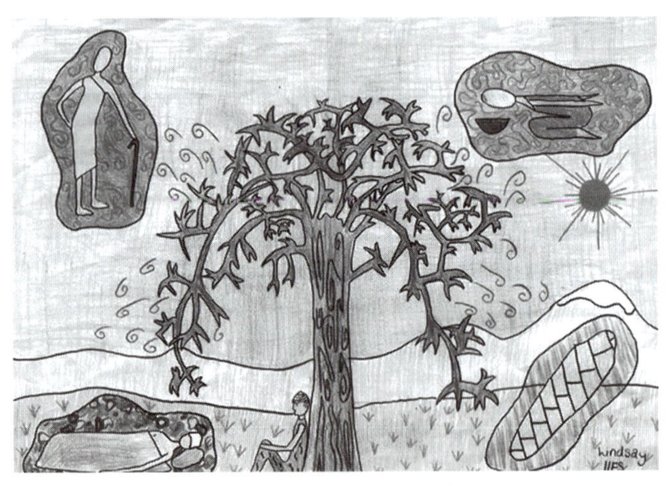

1	King Suddhodana and Queen Maya were excited. They were expecting a baby
2	The Seer told them: 'Your baby will be very special. He may become a great emperor. But if he starts wondering about suffering, he may become an inspiring spiritual leader.'
3	On the night of the full moon, the baby was born. It was a lovely boy. They called him Siddhartha.
4	Tragically, Queen Maya died just seven days after her child was born. Her sister, Siddhartha's aunt, cared for him.
5	The king did not want his child to be a spiritual leader. He made a plan to stop his child ever seeing suffering. He kept the baby prince safe inside the palace.
6	Siddhartha grew up in a world of luxury. He never saw pain or illness. He knew only pleasure.
7	One day as a boy, Siddhartha was taken out of the palace to see the beautiful countryside. But he noticed exhausted peasants working in the fields. He felt uneasy.
8	One day as a boy, he sat all afternoon under a rose apple tree. He felt peaceful, tranquil and calm. It was a special moment, a feeling he wanted to experience more often.
9	When he was 16, he married the beautiful princess Yasodhara from a neighbouring kingdom. The wedding was fabulous, with archery, dancing and a horse riding display.
10	Siddhartha had every luxury and pleasure, but he grew curious, and increasingly dissatisfied with his pleasure palace. He felt a bit restless.
11	One day, aged 29, he persuaded Channa, his chariot driver, to take him out beyond the palace gate secretly, to see the 'real world'. Siddhartha saw four things that changed his life for ever.
12	The first sight was an old person, wrinkled and slow. Siddhartha had never noticed old people. Shocked, he asked Channa: 'Will I grow old? Will I get like that?' Channa nodded.
13	Next he saw an ill person, with a grey, pained face, moaning. Siddhartha was frightened: 'Does illness come to many people? Could that happen to anyone?' Channa nodded again.
14	Then they saw a corpse, a dead body, being taken out to be cremated. Siddhartha knew nothing of death. He watched in silent horror. 'Does everyone die?' he asked. 'Yes', replied Channa.
15	Siddhartha's fourth sight was of a holy man. He walked among the old, the sick and the dead, but he had peace on his face. 'How can he be peaceful? Can I find peace?' Siddhartha wondered.
16	Back at the palace, all his luxury food, the dancing girls and fine wine didn't seem the same. Siddhartha became disgusted with his old life. He brooded and worried, sick of pleasure.
17	The Princess Yasodhara had a baby boy, called Rahula. Even family life seemed less important to Siddhartha than the big question: why is there suffering?
18	Siddhartha decided he must leave the pleasure palace and search for the answer to his question. One night he took a last look at his sleeping princess and baby son, and crept from the palace.
19	Now Siddhartha had no possessions. He asked holy men: 'How can I find the truth?' They taught him to live with nothing. Dressed in rags, eating hardly any food, he followed their path.
20	For 6 years, Siddhartha lived in open forests, learning to control his mind and body. Eating little, he grew very thin. He kept thinking: why do we suffer? But he didn't find an answer to his question.
21	He decided to concentrate on using his mind to answer the question of suffering. He sat still under a tree, determined he would not move until the answer was clear to him.
22	As he sat there, the evil demon Mara tried to distract him. He touched the earth to reassure himself, and thought even more deeply. He wasn't distracted.
23	All night he sat in the deepest meditation and thought. The answer came in the morning. Deeply peaceful, he knew that he was enlightened. He knew the truth at last.
24	Siddhartha sat still, filled with peace and bliss. The story says he sat under the tree for many days, needing nothing. He had found his answer.
25	Siddhartha had now become the Buddha: One who has seen the light.
26	Siddhartha walked to the Deer Park at Sarnath, and met five of his old companions. He taught them the answer to the problem of suffering, and they were also enlightened, and joined him.
27	The next spring Siddhartha returned to his old palace. His son Rahula, now 7, joined his dad. He was accepted by his father as well, who also became a Buddhist.
28	For 45 years, Siddhartha, who was now the Buddha, taught his ideas about the cause of suffering to all who would listen, all over northern India.
29	When he was eighty years old, with many thousands of followers, Siddhartha died. His last moments were full of peace and tranquillity. He did not fear death.
30	The Seer's prediction about the Buddha's inspiring life had come true. Today, 2500 years later, hundreds of millions of Buddhists follow his path all over the world.

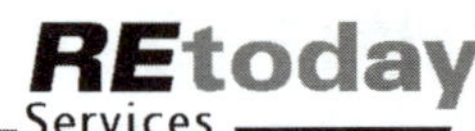

Creating artwork in RE: Judaism

Noah activities for lower primary pupils

This work could build on QCA 2000 unit RC: Who was Noah? It will help pupils to develop key RE skills: name/ talk about (level 1); retell, suggest meanings/respond sensitively (level 2); describe and link (level 3).

- Retell the story of Noah for the pupils and look at a painting of the story, e.g. Rory's picture in this pack. Describe what it shows and how the atmosphere is set, and talk about what the artist might want us to think and feel. Find other examples (internet, picture Bible etc) and use the 'Memory and meaning' strategies (page 8) to explore the picture and story.
- Pupils make a large classroom frieze which retells the story as a sequence. Ask them to think about the materials which will be used, the colours and textures: e.g. both sky and water are blue, but painted bubble wrap might look great for water, while sheets of smooth wrapping paper might make better sky. Rory has made his waterfall entirely from ribbons. Include the flood, a large ark and a rainbow as the main features. Different groups of pupils could take responsibility for different sections or features.

The flood

Theme: judgement, being angry about bad things in the world

- Ask the children, 'What would you like the flood to wash away from the world today?' 'What makes you angry?' 'What do you think are the bad things in the world?'
- Pupils add words and pictures (their own or from magazines) to the flood in the frieze. Experiment with different ways of making it look as if the flood is washing these things away from our world.

The rainbow

Theme: promises

- What would the children like to do in the world? What promises would they like to make to other people, to animals and to the world in order to make a difference? (Talk about things like being kind to animals, picking up litter and saving energy, helping others, giving to charity, being a good friend). Add pupils' promises to the rainbow section of the frieze.

The animals and the people

Theme: being special, recognising our own valuable gifts

- Try basing work on the story *Why Noah Chose the Dove* by Isaac Bashevis Singer (Macmillan, ISBN 0-333-73254-5) In this story each animal says why they think they should be chosen for the ark. Noah takes all of them, because they are all special, and he points out the difference between boasting and recognising our gifts.
- Ask the children, 'What makes you special?' 'What are your own special gifts?' Encourage them to name and identify their individual gifts, and also to suggest nice things about each other. Use a digital camera to take photos of the children and give each of them a speech bubble to fill in and stick on (try using a sentence starter in the speech bubble, e.g. 'I am special because…', or 'I am good at…'). Add the photos and speech bubbles to the ark in the frieze.
- Pupils could go on to think about the character of Noah: what makes him special? What are his qualities and gifts? In groups, they could design and create a Noah figure to add to the ark, made in collage and using different colours and textures from magazines and newspapers to show his personality. E.g. if they want to show that he was kind, they might show him wearing a fluffy jumper. If they want to show that he was gritty and determined, they might use sandpaper for his face.

Esther and Purim activities for upper primary pupils

The following activities enable pupils to develop the skills of responding sensitively (level 2), describing and making links (level 3), showing understanding and applying ideas (level 4).

- Read the story of Esther with the class, or watch a video. Pupils could find out how Jews celebrate the festival of Purim today (e.g. www.holidays.net/purim is an interactive website with lots of practical ideas).
- Split pupils into groups of 3. Enlarge and give out the cards below and provide a similar Bulls Eye diagram. Ask pupils in groups to arrange the cards on the diagram 3 times according to: 1. What is important to Esther? 2. What is important to Jewish people at Purim? 3. What is important to me? Include some blank cards for pupils' own ideas.

The 10 commandments	Justice	Freedom	My religious faith
Praying	Worshipping God	Keeping the Sabbath holy	Being respected
Equality	Hamantashan/ purim cookies	Giving to the poor	Being admired
Family	Graggers/ noisemakers	Beauty and good looks	Telling the truth
Celebrating & Remembering	Dressing up/masks	Fasting	Special places
Party games	Defeating evil	Being safe	Special people
Other people	Bravery	Me	Special stories

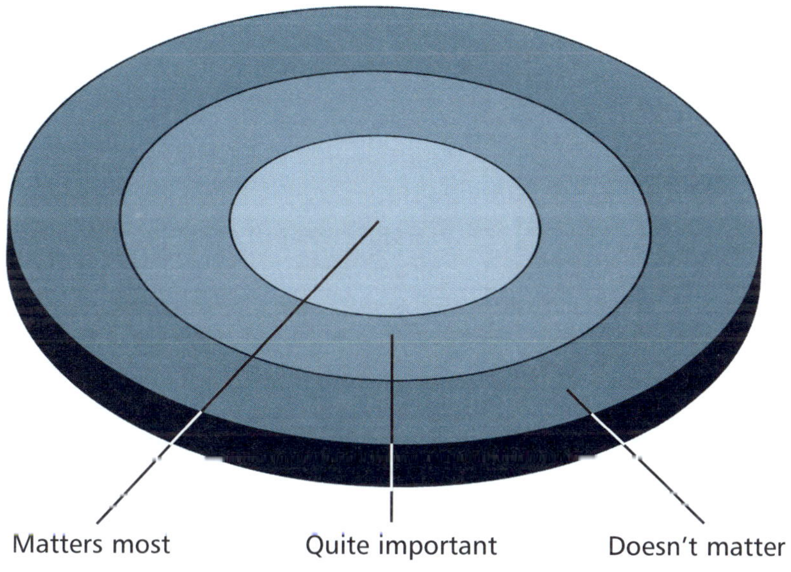

Activity One: Spirit sculptures

Ask pupils to think of things to symbolise what is most important to Esther: e.g. a lion might be a symbol of bravery, a flag might be a symbol of freedom. Provide art materials and ask pupils to depict Esther's spirit using a selection of images as symbols, or ask them to collect objects which could be used as symbols and create an 'Esther's spirit' sculpture in a display area.

They could repeat this activity for 'What is most important for me?', creating symbolic self-portraits or sculptures

Activity Two: A heroic moment

The story of Esther is important for Jews today because of the holocaust. **More able pupils** aiming for level 5 could look at what happened during the holocaust and **explain** why Esther has become a Jewish heroine. Pupils could choose a key moment from Esther's story to depict in their own artwork to **express their views**, modernised, or set in a different time or culture (e.g. during the Second World War), or in a country which has recently experienced genocide (e.g. Rwanda). Pupils could write a paragraph explaining their work

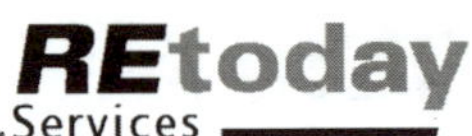

Creating artwork in RE: Hinduism

Activity One: My spirit in technicolor

- Ask pupils to look carefully at the pictures in the pack by Curtis, Kate and Holly (3, 5, 7).
- Remove the pictures and ask pupils to try to draw one from memory, using pastel, crayons or coloured pencils. What did they remember most clearly? What is the picture about?
- Read what the artists say about their pictures. They all use both light and dark colours to express their 'spirit'. Why is this?
- Provide each pupil with a sheet of paper with the following words down one side: Happy, Sad, Peaceful, Angry, Thoughtful, Playful, Quiet, Forgiving, Bad, Confused, Good, Kind, Selfish, Joyful, Noisy. Opposite the word, they write the colour (using the colour) that they associate with the word. They can add other words and colours if they want to.
- Pupils then draw themselves, using the colours that describe how they see themselves, and how they are feeling right now. They should draw their picture 'inside out' i.e. as they are on the inside, rather than a self-portrait of the outside.
- They write a short explanation of how they have used colour to describe themselves.

Creation Yantra

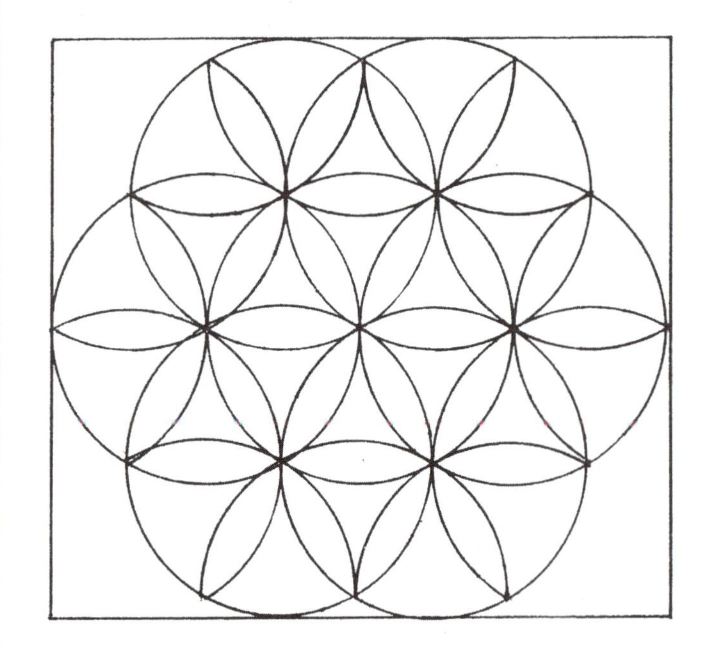

N.B. See the guidelines for colouring mandalas on the next page.

Activity Two: Colour and design in Hinduism

Mandalas are sacred geometric patterns, symbolising the unity of all things in the universe. They are used as a focus for meditation. The designs can be quite simple or very complex. By colouring the pattern, many beautiful, different designs are produced, while at the same time being exactly the same.

- Give each pupil an enlarged copy of the Creation Yantra which is based on the lotus flower.
- Pupils colour the mandala, thinking carefully about the colours they want to use (remembering Activity One). Which colours and feelings do they associate with 'creation?' (Larger copies of the mandala allow more creativity with, for example, scrunched-up tissue paper, coloured sand and glue, small squares of cut-up coloured magazines.)
- As a stimulus, try reading this Hindu creation myth as a guided visualisation:

Before the world was created, there was nothing but water. Out of the murky dark waters, a single lotus flower had begun to grow with Brahma the creator sitting in it. The Lord Vishnu spoke to Brahma and told him it was time for the world to be created. Brahma divided the lotus into three parts. The first became heaven, the second become the earth and the third was the sky. A faint sound grew louder... AUM...AUM... AUM, until everywhere was filled with it. Suddenly the world was full of newly created creatures. Brahma divided his body into two parts, and from one part he made man, from the other he made woman.

The lotus flower

The lotus flower is an important symbol in Hinduism. It grows out of the dirty, muddy water yet the flowers remain untainted by the dirt. It has become a symbol for:

- the person who is seeking moksha – release from the cycle of birth, death and rebirth (samsara). Once the atman (soul) attains perfection or purity (symbolised by the lotus flower) it leaves worldly attachments and wrong doings (the murky water) behind. A person's actions (karma) determine their rebirth.
- creation in Hindu mythology: see the story on page 20.
- life, beauty, prosperity, fertility and purity. Many gods and goddesses are pictured sitting on a lotus flower – a symbol of their divinity – and holding a lotus flower, symbolising their purity.

Activity Three: Understanding atman, karma, samsara and moksha through the symbol of the lotus flower

- Describe for pupils what these terms mean to Hindus.
- Give each pupil enlarged versions of the lotus flower and leaf templates below. On each petal they write good actions; on the leaves they write bad actions. Talk about what they might include in each category. They could colour the flowers: which colours might represent good deeds, and which might represent bad?
- Create a 3D display: cut out the lotus flowers, lay one set of petals on top of another to create a fuller flower, secure to a straw. Push the other end of the straw through a piece of paper or card which has been coloured to look like dirty water and secure it underneath. Place the lotus leaves near the straw stem. Display these with pupils' written explanations of their work, making links between the meaning of the flowers and Hindu beliefs.

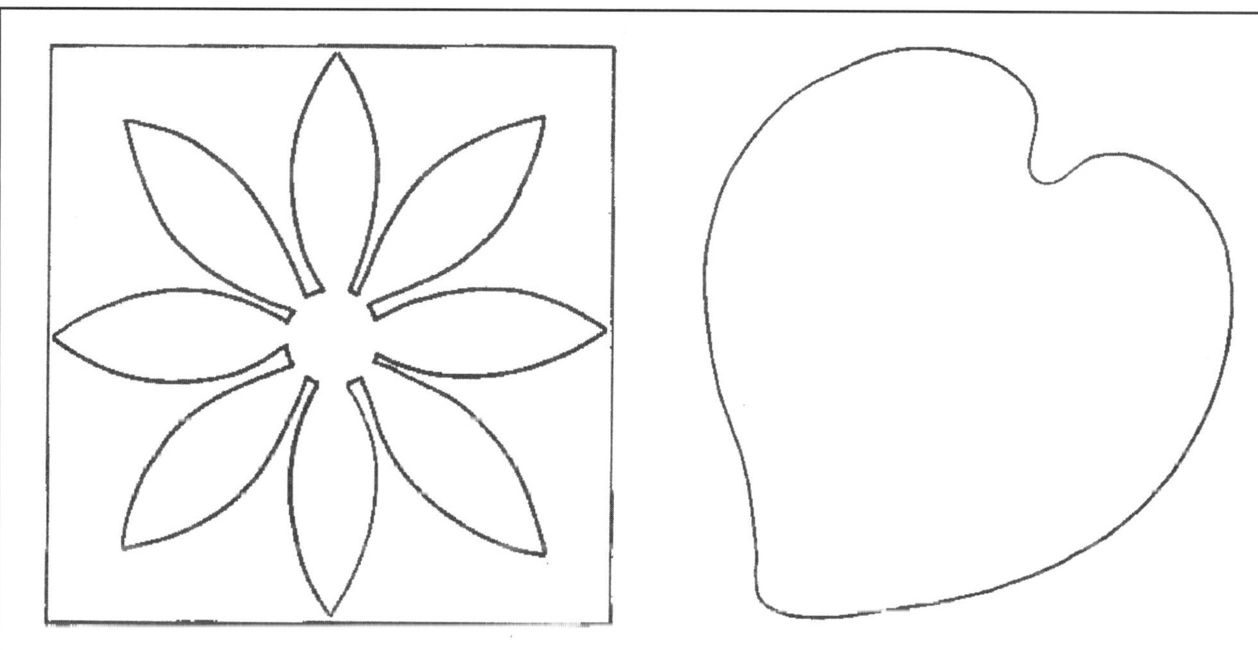

Guidelines for colouring mandalas: start at the centre and work outwards if the mandala is to bring out and express what is innermost, or start at the edges and work towards the centre if the mandala is to help identify and reveal hidden innermost thoughts and feelings. Colours should be chosen instinctively and the finished mandala studied thoughtfully and reflectively: what meaning might the colours have?

This mandala work will help pupils to develop key 'learning from religion' skills as they respond sensitively (level 2) to the creation story, make links (level 3) between their feelings and the colours they choose, or apply ideas about mandalas to their own creative work (level 4).

 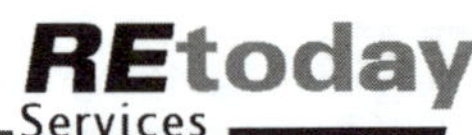

Assessment: What do pupils learn from the spiritual? How do pupils show their achievements?

An 'assessment for learning' approach to art in RE

The next three pages give a flexible format by which children aged 7 or 11 can show their responses to some works of religious or spiritual art. You could use some of the 8 picture cards in this pack as a stimulus for the work, or gather a set of images of your own

What sorts of stimuli can be used? Try:

- Postcards: ask pupils to choose one that makes them think, or gives them a mysterious or puzzled feeling, and they will pick up the spirituality of the art.
- *Picturing Jesus:* two packs of 16 picture cards (see Resources page). They refer to Christian spirituality globally and to the narratives of the biblical gospels.
- Nature and spiritual ideas: use 'natural world' pictures – collect a set of 40 or more to make this work really well. Animals, views, sunsets, wonders of nature, microscopic pictures and many more are suitable. Old *National Geographic* magazines are just one source among many.
- Justice for all people: collect some images of injustice for this. Use OXFAM, Christian Aid or Tear Fund catalogues and Sunday newspaper supplements for worldwide images. Ask pupils to choose one image and write the story of one person in it, as they imagine it.

'I can…' – tools for assessing RE

Using 'I can' statements helps pupils to see what the teacher is looking for and is invaluable in interpreting the 8-level scale for RE. Here are some for these activities, aimed at levels 1–4.

Level 1

- I can recognise something spiritual in a picture.
- I can talk about my feelings.
- I can talk about some puzzling questions.

Level 2

- I can suggest a meaning in an image.
- I can respond sensitively to what others say about a spiritual image.
- I can ask good questions about spiritual feelings.

Level 3

- I can describe how a picture can be spiritual for some people.
- I can make a link between my ideas about hope, love or fear and one of the pictures used.
- I can make a link between the images I've looked at and some questions that puzzle me.

Level 4

- I can show that I understand the impact of a religious work of art on a believer.
- I can apply an idea about belief in God or about what matters most to an image I have studied.
- I can suggest the answers an artist might give to my questions about his/her work.

How to use the frames

On the next pages, you will find an outline for a self-assessment for 7-year-olds, and then one for 11-year-olds. Use these with any works of religious art you use as a learning resource. In each case, there are five steps to the activity: 1. Sketching a work of art from a religious or spiritual source; 2. Commenting on the art work; 3. Making a work of art themselves; 4. Commenting on their own work; 5. Evaluating their own work by selecting 'I can…' statements that apply to their performance.

What can we learn from looking at some art work in RE? For 7-year-olds:

The picture I have been learning about is called…

What I like about it is…

Here is my sketch of the picture:

My thoughts
I can see…

I have been wondering…

I would like to ask the painter…

This picture is important because…

In my picture I have drawn…

My picture is spiritual because…

4 words that say what makes my picture special:

My tiny spiritual work of art:

Highlight the sentences that you **can do** in green. Mark in red any you **can't do**.

- I can talk about the painting I have been looking at.
- I can say what the picture shows.
- I can tell the story of the picture.
- I can say what the picture means for myself.
- I can be sensitive when I describe my picture.

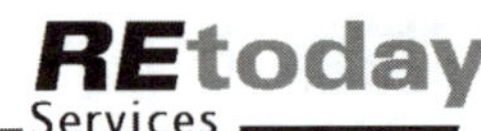

What can we learn from looking at some art work in RE? For 11-year-olds:

The picture I have been learning about is called…

The artist is…

3 things that I like about it are…

Here is my sketch of the picture:

My thoughts

My five words to describe the picture are…

I would like to ask the painter…

This is a religious picture because…

The picture makes an impact by…

In my picture I have expressed…

This is a spiritual picture because…

5 words to make sense of my picture are:

My tiny spiritual work of art:

Highlight the sentences that you **can do** in green. Mark in red any you **can't do**.

- I can describe the painting I've been using.
- I can give a reason why a believer might value this painting.
- I can make a link between this painting and another art work that I like.
- I can suggest three good questions to ask the artist about faith and art.
- I can use the images to think about a puzzling question and suggest an answer of my own.